Life in Kindergarten

A Teacher Remembers

Glenda Munson

Gotham Books

30 N Gould St.
Ste. 20820, Sheridan, WY 82801
https://gothambooksinc.com/

Phone: 1 (307) 464-7800

© 2025 *Glenda Munson*. All rights reserved.

No part of this book may be reproduced, stored in a retrieval system, or transmitted by any means without the written permission of the author.

Published by Gotham Books (May 23, 2025)

ISBN: 979-8-3484-9420-9 (H)
ISBN: 979-8-3484-9418-6 (P)
ISBN: 979-8-3484-9419-3 (E)

Because of the dynamic nature of the Internet, any web addresses or links contained in this book may have changed since publication and may no longer be valid.

The views expressed in this work are solely those of the author and do not necessarily reflect the views of the publisher, and the publisher hereby disclaims any responsibility for them.

Table of Contents

Introduction to Kindergarten 1

A Career Choice 4

The First Time 10

Ralph 15

Room to Grow 18

Jack and Jacky 21

Messy Memories 26

A Time for Slime 31

Paula 34

Kelli 39

The Principal 41

Change 47

A Treetop View 51

Ready or Not 57

Of Mice and Kids 61

Kevin 65

A Small World 68

Job Sharing 74

College Park 84

Welcome to Wilson 87

Danny 92

Conference Time	96
Miranda	100
Another Kevin	103
A Room Divided	106
Room 11	110
Stories to Go	117
Sean	120
Mariana	125
Arlene	129
Paper Dolls	134
Leave of Absence	137
The Bell Choir	141
Nora	146
Off We Go	150
Down the Chimney	156
Daisy	160
Alena	165
Thematic Instruction	169
Lindy and the Angel	177
Gerardo	181
Valentines	186
The Language Barrier	193
The Number Line	199
Jesus	202

Dedication

This book is dedicated to my:

darling daughter,

Dana Quebbemann,

the kindergarten teacher

to whom I passed

the torch.

Introduction to Kindergarten

In August of 1945, on the day of my fifth birthday, Emperor Hirohito surrendered his sword, and the world entered a period of peace. During the only years I could remember, the world was at war. My father was in the Navy, stationed in San Diego, California, working as a machinist at the shipyard. Now the war was over! As we drove around the city, we could hear church bells ringing everywhere in a joyous chorus. The streets were full of sailors in uniform, laughing and cheering. The world was at peace. No more listening for air raid sirens or huddling in the dark house during blackouts. That same birthday made me eligible to enter the unknown world of kindergarten. What would it be like? Was it a new thing to fear?

We lived in naval housing in nearby Chula Vista, where I started school. Memories of the teacher are vague, a lady with short brown hair and a nice smile. That first day began a little scarily for me because I fell asleep on my mat during nap time. When I awoke, I realized that the other children were already gathered in front of the teacher. I remember being very embarrassed to join them. Should I pretend to still be sleeping? Bravely, I joined them because the teacher was reading aloud from a book. Kindergarten was a place of stories!

Only fragments of memory remain from that year. At Thanksgiving time, we learned about Indians. We made paper headbands with colored construction paper feathers. Our drums were made by covering a Quaker oats cereal box with paper and painting it. It was exciting as we danced in a circle wearing the headdresses and beating drums. Another recollection is of an art project at Christmas. We were each provided an empty matchbox that slid open like a little drawer. We covered it with colored paper and glued sparkly sequins on top. I thought it was an object of artistic beauty and was proud to gift it to my mom. Kindergarten was a place to create!

When my father got out of the Navy, we moved back to Alhambra, where I enrolled in first grade. I did not like it nearly as well. We had to sit in the same desk all day and we never danced with drums. One day, as a treat, the teacher let us take our recess in the kindergarten yard instead of on the big playground. It was a separate fenced area with grass and a shade tree. There were swings and a slide, but I was content to sit on the ground and use a hammer to pound nails into a railroad tie. Construction was a favorite thing I enjoyed doing at home with my carpenter uncle. To my great disappointment, we were never again allowed to visit the kindergarten yard.

You know how some recollections remain? Despite the passage of time, you can call them up again, like an old photo that captures a moment and freezes it. One such picture remains a memory for me. I am standing outside the fence that encloses that kindergarten yard. My first-grade feet are firmly planted outside on an expanse of blacktop where multiple classes of children are running around, including the bully in second grade, who routinely threatens to beat me up. The big playground also contains the bars that are too high to reach, where I try unsuccessfully to learn to hang by my knees. In the picture, my fingers are curled around that chain link fence. I am gazing wistfully through the wire at the soft grass beneath the tree and wishing I was once again in that yard. It is the peaceful world of kindergarten. I can still feel that longing. Perhaps that was the moment a seed was sewn, to flower in the future.

My first day of kindergarten

A Career Choice

What do you want to be when you grow up? There was a time when I would have answered, "Either a cowboy or a carpenter," but later I discovered that wasn't an acceptable choice for a girl. When I graduated high school, I had no idea what I wanted to do next. Should I look for a job? Definitely not as a receptionist, a salesclerk, or a secretary. I had tried those during vacations, but I desired something less routine and more interesting. I decided to attend Pasadena City College while figuring out a career choice.

I began as an art major. That was the subject I liked most in high school. Perhaps an artist would be an enjoyable job. However, I soon began to question that. I did not like the instructor, or my art class assignments. Also, the idea of a regular paycheck was appealing to me. That doesn't necessarily come with being an artist.

I changed my major to English, my other favorite subject. English literature was appealing as I had always loved to read. I also did well in English Composition class as creative writing was fun. I had met a boy, Bob, on the first day of classes. He was a pre-med major and had difficulty in the English class that we shared. I began to tutor him occasionally and he, in turn, helped me in our physics class. I started to think about teaching English someday, perhaps at the college level.

Eventually, Bob invited me to his home for dinner and introduced me to his parents. His mother was a kindergarten teacher. She shared with me how much she enjoyed teaching. She also enumerated some advantages that I hadn't thought of. She said, "Unlike in many other careers, you are both a working parent and a stay-at-home mom, as your teaching schedule is compatible with that of your children. You are at home with them all summer and on school holidays." She also pointed out that, with tenure, you have a secure position, and a retirement pension that exceeds that of Social Security.

I continued to date Bob. During our second year of college, his mom invited me to visit her kindergarten classroom. I confided to Marion one reservation about teaching English. I couldn't see how my love of art and dance (subjects I was still taking courses in) would fit into that career. She said one of the reasons she loved teaching elementary was because music, (both song and dance), and art and literature, were all part of the daily program. Furthermore, she explained that you could be especially creative in kindergarten because the curriculum was not mandated until first grade. The choice of activities and themes to incorporate was up to you. I began to see some advantages of the opposite end of the spectrum from college.

A concern about elementary level was that I was an only child. I had never been around young children. They seemed as foreign to me as creatures from another planet. I wondered if I would like them. "Come and visit my classroom!" she encouraged. I went. Washington Elementary was a beautiful old school with an ornate stone exterior. Her cheerful classroom was a spacious, bright corner room with tall windows. To my surprise, the children accepted me immediately. They were welcoming and surrounded me with love. I observed Marion as she used a hand puppet to tell a story in a dramatic voice. Kindergarten suited her personality because she was always happy and cheerful. "I want to be like that," I thought.

I joined the games on the shady playground and the folk dancing in the room. The children and I made a craft project and painted at the easels. I read a story aloud. As I sat there, surrounded by totally absorbed little listening faces, I decided that reading *Red Riding Hood* aloud was better than expounding about *Madame Bovary*. It was so pleasant that it didn't seem like work. I had entered another world. It might be inhabited by little aliens, but it was a planet filled with creativity and endless variety. It crackled with excitement. Everything was being experienced for the first time. It was a warm, happy world fueled by milk and graham crackers, brimming with learning. I had glimpsed the place where I wanted to spend my life. I decided to become a kindergarten teacher!

Bob and I graduated from Pasadena City College and transferred to Marion's alma mater, U.C.L.A. I majored in Elementary Education and English. Now, Marion and I not only talked, we chattered. She bubbled about kindergarten activities. She was my mentor. When I took a class in Elementary Music, she taught me little songs and cute finger plays. She encouraged me to learn to play the piano. When I enrolled in Art for Classroom Teachers, she provided me with samples and directions for art activities. When I took Children's Literature, she shared her favorite storybooks. She was a wonderful resource.

Part of the curriculum required for the final year at U.C.L.A. was a semester of classroom participation. There was a demonstration school located on campus. I was lucky enough to be assigned there. I felt even luckier when I found out that my placement was in the kindergarten class I requested. It required observing and assisting the teacher. The object was to familiarize the college student with that grade level. The teacher allowed me to read at story time and to lead art lessons and games.

The room was spacious. One whole wall was sliding glass doors that connected to a patio and the kindergarten yard. There was no blacktop, just a large expanse of lush green lawn sloping down to a stream, lined with tall eucalyptus trees, as the school is built on the edge of a ravine that runs through the center of the university. Paint easels were set up on the patio. The lawn was scattered with colorful toys and in the center was an actual old wooden boat for the children to climb on. There was even a live goat allowed to roam the yard and graze on the grass.

My class was every Tuesday and Thursday morning. What I mainly observed is that kindergarten is a happy place. In one memory that stays with me, I am standing on the lawn outside the classroom. It is a beautiful morning, and the sunlight is sifting through the leaves of the tall trees in the ravine. A child is painting at an easel on the patio, laughing children are rolling a ball on the lawn, others are climbing on the boat. One boy is petting the goat. In that moment, I am content. I am once again in kindergarten.

During the final semester of senior year, students are placed in two student teaching assignments. They are required to be done in different grades. My first assignment was a second grade at the university demonstration school. When I reported on the first day to meet my master teacher, I found her marching down the hall carrying a large coffee maker. I told her who I was. She replied, "Oh, just go on down the hall. The kids will be coming in from recess. Just introduce yourself and have them get on their rest mats. I'm setting up for the faculty luncheon. I'll be along later," and off she hurried.

I located the classroom in time to witness a herd of kids rush into the room, no line, just a stampede. The noise level was so high I doubt if many heard me introduce myself, and of course my directions to get on their mats carried no authority. By shouting, I finally got all but one girl settled. She remained on her hands and knees with her head poked through the rungs of a classroom chair. When I told her that boys and girls needed to get on their rest mats, she replied loudly, "I'm not a girl. I'm a cow in a stanchion!" (They were studying the dairy.) Although I favorably noted her precocious vocabulary, her remark generated uproarious laughter from the class which, of course, was when the teacher walked in. From there on, it was all downhill. The teacher had a casual attitude toward classroom behavior. It was her style and worked for her. I, on the other hand, had to constantly struggle to maintain class control. I found second grade to be a year when children begin to value the approval of their peers over that of the teacher. It is a time when some begin their academic career as class clown, constantly trying for a laugh, being both noisy and disruptive. I was happy when it was time to leave second grade behind me.

My next student teaching assignment was off campus in the Los Angeles School District. Nora Sterry Elementary was an old school, first established in the 1800's. It co-operated with U.C.L.A. in their teacher training program. I was assigned to kindergarten which was in a separate structure from the other school buildings. When I met my master teacher, she gave me a tour of what resembled a charming old house. In the entryway was an old wooden staircase that led to the second floor, where she had her office. The main classroom was a large space that might once have been a living room. It was here where the children sat on the rug for lessons and story time. The rest of the room was used for block play or music. Through a large archway was an attached room that perhaps had been a dining room. It was now used for nap time. The children spread their mats out on the hardwood floor. Around the walls were shelves with science exhibits: birds' nests, rocks, shells, and terrariums. In the back of the house was a bathroom, and a kitchen where snacks were prepared and delivered to the nap room when they awoke.

Many of the children were of the Japanese heritage prevalent in the area. I don't know if it was a cultural thing, or perhaps the training of the master teacher, but this class was extremely attentive and well behaved. They would sit cross-legged on the rug so quietly that I almost had stage fright presenting my lessons. What a contrast to second grade.

I loved that the kindergarten was in a separate house. It felt like a cozy home. Later I found out that it was actually built as a schoolhouse in 1914 to replace the original structure when it burnt down. I enjoyed my student teaching in that environment. I couldn't wait to spend my future in the peaceful world of kindergarten.

The First Time

Life is filled with firsts, beginnings that live on in memory. I had just graduated from UCLA in June, with a bachelor's degree and a Primary teaching credential. So, in August of 1961, I was finally qualified to begin my career. Sitting in an orientation meeting for new teachers at the South San Francisco Unified School District, I was preparing to start my first job.

The room was filled with newly hired teachers, waiting for their assignments. I sat next to a young woman about my age. (I had turned twenty-one a week ago.) She looked friendly, perhaps also a little anxious. We listened attentively as district officials introduced themselves and welcomed us. They passed out a handbook with information, asking us to look it over during the refreshment break. I chatted with the girl next to me and we shared our backgrounds. She too was about to start her first teaching job and was thrilled. I had a feeling we would become friends, as we had a lot in common. I had just been married in June. She was also a newlywed. We confided to each other that we were also pregnant.

We proceeded to study the handbook. She leaned over and pointed to a section that referred to pregnancy. She looked worried. "It says here you must immediately inform the district when you become pregnant. It doesn't disclose how long you are allowed to work." She decided to go during lunch and tell them that she was pregnant. She did not want to be in trouble later for keeping it secret.

I debated whether to do the same thing. I almost always follow rules exactly, but in this case, there was too much at stake. My new husband was just beginning medical school at the University of California. Getting pregnant on our honeymoon had not been in our plans. My teaching income was to be our only means of support. Without it, he would have to give up the dream of becoming a doctor. We needed that paycheck!

I turned to the girl and said, "I am not ready to tell yet. Please don't mention me in your discussion." She promised she would keep my confidence and left her things with me, while she went to the office. I ate lunch and worried about whether I was making the right decision. After a while she returned with tears in her eyes.

"They won't let me begin the school year," she said. When they learned her news, they had terminated her employment on the spot. They did not want to employ a pregnant teacher. The girl left, upset, and crying and I never saw her again.

I decided to keep my secret as long as I could. School would start soon in September. I really needed to make it at least to that first paycheck on October first. Bob and I had lived free with his parents for the first few weeks of our marriage. We managed to save every penny of our wedding present money, which totaled $500. With medical school set to begin at the end of August, we drove the old Studebaker that Bob inherited from his grandfather, to San Francisco. There we rented a one-bedroom apartment for $100 a month. To furnish it we spent another $100 to purchase a mattress and box springs set. (The store threw in a bed frame and bedspread for free.) That left $300 dollars to cover food and medical books.

The school district gave me my first teaching assignment. It was to be in a first grade. I had asked for kindergarten, but any job was a cause for celebration. The elementary school was in a nice neighborhood of South San Francisco, surrounded by neat middle-class homes. Most of the school was set on the top of a hill, but the first-grade classrooms were in a separate building down at the bottom.

My classroom was the first room. It was medium sized with thirty little desks, six rows of five, all facing a blackboard at the front of the room. The desk for the teacher was off in the corner. Right away that set up made me uncomfortable. I pictured the large kindergarten of my student teaching, where little ones sat gathered around you on a carpet, and little circular tables where you did art or served milk and graham crackers. It had been more of a playroom.

Instead, on the first day of school, I stood anxiously in front of the class. The children sat in their neat rows staring up at me expectantly, like I knew exactly what to do. Inside, I felt more than a little panicked, experiencing stage fright. Not only was this my first day of teaching, but as an only child I had not grown up around children. At twenty-one I had only technically been an adult for three weeks. How could they leave me completely in charge and responsible for thirty little human beings? Didn't they know any better? Nevertheless, I somehow gathered my courage and began to teach.

The children were very nice, but I can't say I liked first grade much. My unfavorite time of the day was a large block of time for reading instruction. Reading was still taught the same way it had been when I was in first grade, from the same readers that featured Dick and Jane.

I divided the class into three groups of ten children who would take turns coming to the back of the classroom. They sat in a reading circle with me, holding books on their laps. We would go around the group, giving each child a chance to read a line. Each day I carefully followed the lesson plans in the manual. They told me which new word to introduce and even what to say. Each child struggled to read slowly, "See Jane run, run Dick run!" It was like pulling teeth! Then it was time to repeat the same thing again with the next group and then once more. It was about as exciting as watching grass grow. I found it hard to stay awake.

Other subjects were better and somewhat more enjoyable. October finally arrived, and I collected my first paycheck. It was a cause for celebration. We could survive another month. Still, I kept my secret. I was over three months pregnant by then and I stopped wearing clothes with tight waistbands, opting for jumpers or elastic waistbands. Fortunately, I never experienced any morning sickness and I felt strong and healthy. I thought I could probably make it to the November paycheck before I started to show. Finally, at Halloween, I sat down with my principal in his office and told him that I was expecting. It was a scary moment. I was worried about his reaction. As it turned out he was very nice, but explained that district policy was to replace me as soon as possible. He did comment that I had been doing a good job. I think he guessed our financial situation, as he seemed to drag his feet in finding a new teacher. In mid-November he came to me and said that my replacement was to be another medical student's wife from out of the area. She could not arrive until Christmas vacation. Would I mind teaching until then? (*Would I mind getting a December paycheck?*) I think the joy on my face was an answer.

In December, he came to me again and said there was a complication. The new teacher would not be available until the end of the semester. They could look for a different replacement, or, on his recommendation, the district would let me teach until the end of February. I would need to bring a note from my doctor that it was alright and stating my due date. My baby was due on March 17th. My doctor was cool; he fudged a little and wrote April 1st on my note. (He was, by the way, treating me free, as medical courtesy extended to the families of student doctors.)

This development was a great relief. I would continue to receive paychecks through the end of the semester and the summer pay that had been withheld would see us through the month of March. (Bob would get a paying grant to experiment on rats during spring break.) It was a reprieve, even if temporary. With care we could make it until the end of term in May and sublet our apartment for the summer.

Somehow, I was making it through this frantic time of **firsts**: my **first** time as a wife, my **first** time moving 500 miles away from family, my **first** apartment, my **first** year as an adult, my **first** teaching job, my frightening **first** day, my **first** pregnancy, my **first** time to become a mother, and finally, my **first** experience in **first** grade!

Ralph

I remember little about the students in my very first class. It was, after all, almost sixty years ago. Those children are now old enough to be on social security. I hope they are well and enjoying life. Their class was one of three first grades in the school where I began teaching. The students had been grouped by ability the previous year on the recommendation of their kindergarten teacher.

The class across the hall from me was composed of children who were expected to earn a grade of A or B. My class contained the children who were deemed average, and the third class down the hall was called the Junior Primary for kids who might need two years of kindergarten/first grade, usually the younger ones.

The purpose of grouping was so that the teacher could more accurately tailor her instruction to the instructional level of her class. My average group seemed to have the advantage of being calm and attentive. There was not a troublemaker in the group. There were a couple children who seemed to shine and catch on more quickly, but for the most part I think they had been sorted well.

Each morning at the beginning of our day, we had a few minutes of sharing time when I would call on different students to show and talk about an item that they had brought from home. It helped me get to know them and it fostered their verbal ability. I could often turn whatever they brought into a learning opportunity. For example, if they shared a pinecone, a leaf, or a cocoon, it could spark a science lesson.

I remember one day when a boy named Ralph brought in a football to share. He was very proud of it as he showed it to the group and told them that he wanted to be a football player someday. Ralph was somewhat slow in learning to read. Reading was then taught using mostly a method called sight recognition. You introduced a new word and repeated it over and over. I decided it couldn't hurt to also introduce some phonics, to help them sound out new words. I would play word games with the first consonant of whatever they brought to share. So, this morning we talked about the football starting with letter F and the sound it made. The class volunteered lots of words that began with that sound, but not Ralph. Since it was his turn, I asked him to think of an F word (now don't get excited, back then even the teacher had never heard that word.) Anyway, Ralph remained silent, scrunching up his face as he thought hard. "It sounds like fffff..." I prompted, making the angry cat sound. He still looked befuddled. To give him an extra hint I pointed down at his feet on the floor.

He looked pained as he tried to guess a word and then he blurted out, "Fffff...Shoe!" It sounded almost like a sneeze. I couldn't help laughing. Each time I teach phonics I remember "Ffffshoe!" and sturdy little Ralph. I wonder if perhaps he did become a football player.

For some reason my memories of Ralph are all connected with sharing time. On another day, he could hardly wait to share and kept waving his hand in the air. I called on him and he walked to the front of the class. I did not see that he had anything to show. Then he reached into his pocket and pulled out a lump of aluminum foil. With a smile he began to unwrap it. His smile faded as he discovered nothing inside but a few drops of water, which trickled down onto the floor. His big blue eyes welled up with tears as he looked at me bewildered. Gone was whatever wonderful thing he had brought to share! Finally, between his sobs I found out that his mom had wrapped up a pocketful of ice cubes. *What a smart mom,* I thought. We had been studying the changing states of water and this was the perfect lead in to another science lesson. Ralph cheered up when the children began to discuss with interest what had happened to his sharing.

On another day Ralph marched to the front of the class looking a little pale and then just stood there, seemingly tongue-tied. When he said nothing, I prodded, "Ralph?" For just a second, he looked a little panicked then opened his mouth and threw up! But this was no ordinary barf. He was projectile vomiting what looked like a great quantity of blood. It was like something out of a horror movie. On second glance, it was too bright a red to be blood; it looked more like paint. I immediately sent Ralph to the school nurse and requested the custodian to clean up my room. Fortunately, it was almost recess time. During that break I rushed to the office to check on Ralph, only to find chaos. Ralph's two older siblings were also in the nurse's office and there were now three children throwing up red paint! They were in the process of calling the mother to come to the school. The secretary took me aside and confided that one of the older children had said their mother made them all drink something that morning. "The nurse is unsure what it is," she whispered, "We are concerned it might be poison! So far the principal has not called the police."

"*Oh no,*" I thought, "*not the mother who sent the ice. She is so nice!*" But recess was over, and I had to rush back to my class. By lunchtime all was sorted out. The mother had come to the office and explained that she had administered deworming medicine to all three children. A call to their doctor had confirmed her account. The children were now feeling fine but had been sent home for the day. They had all shared a little too much!

Room to Grow

I was allowed to finish the semester in first grade. The baby was born on March 21st, the first day of Spring. Somehow my husband and I made it financially through his first year of medical school, just barely. By the time the term ended at the end of May, we were broke. We sublet our apartment for the summer to another med student, and with our new baby, returned to Pasadena to live free with Bob's parents. Bob had obtained a grant from USC to do research on rats, so he made a small income over the summer. I no longer had employment but was taking care of our baby. We had no idea how we would survive in the Fall. Was a second year of medical school even going to be possible? If so, I needed a job.

One afternoon toward the end of summer, the phone in Pasadena rang. It was a long- distance call from my principal. He had learned that I had reapplied at the South San Francisco School District. He said he would like to have me back on staff, but unfortunately, he had no first-grade openings at this time. "Would you consider teaching kindergarten?" he asked. I could have exploded with joy! Not only was it a needed job offer, but that was the grade level I had always wanted to teach. I was thrilled to answer him with an emphatic "yes."

When I returned to Buri Buri Elementary School in September, it was as a kindergarten teacher! My new room was very different from the first grade where I had taught last year. For one thing, it might be a lower grade level, but the classroom was a step up, literally. It sat at the top of the hill, close to the office, connected by a covered walkway. No more trudging up the steep hill from the first-grade wing on wind driven rainy days. The kindergarten was a separate building containing only two large classrooms connected by a teacher's workroom and two bathrooms.

When I walked in, I was pleasantly surprised by how large my room was (at least twice as big as the first-grade room.) The ceilings were very high. One wall was nothing but windows, with a view overlooking the green hills of South San Francisco. Another wall had a long built-in easel, with cupboards underneath for paint storage. A row of transom windows high above flooded the room with light. It was a bright cheerful place that would be my home for the next three years while Bob attended medical school.

There were several long worktables with tiny chairs in the middle of the room, but it was so large that there was still a huge open area for block play or dance. In one corner was the playhouse, complete with a tiny stove and refrigerator and a bed full of dolls. In the cozy corner by the windows was a rectangular area rug on the floor and to my great delight, a piano.

It was customary, at that time, for kindergarten teachers to play the piano. I had never had lessons, but I had taken a course in piano during college. I learned to read some music and accompany it with chords. Now, I could sit at the piano after school and teach myself the simple songs I needed to play for music time. The teacher's desk stood facing out across the room where I could observe all the areas, (should I ever have a moment to sit down.)

The kindergarten day lasted two and a half hours for each session, a morning, and an afternoon class. Opening consisted of roll call, flag salute, calendar, sharing, and a short lesson. It was followed by a block of time when children could choose to work around the room. There was a daily craft activity at the tables, painting at the easels, block play, playhouse, a science exploration area and a variety of games and puzzles. Work time was followed by nutrition. The custodian would deliver a tray of tiny cartons of milk to serve with graham crackers.

This was followed by an outdoor time, recess and P.E. When the children came inside from play, they would get a padded plastic rest mat from the stack against the wall, place it on the floor and lie down. I would put on a soothing record and they would nap for ten minutes. They were usually tired enough to do this quietly, but they also had another incentive. I had a sparkly "magic" fairy wand and when I tapped them gently on the head they could wake up and go sit on the rug. For some reason they loved this, and the fairy only tapped you if you were very, very quiet.

On the rug we had story time (my favorite time of the day) and music. I would play simple songs on the piano, or put on records, or strum the autoharp. There was plenty of room to move about the huge room. We lumbered about as elephants or walked like penguins with our toes turned out, or galloped as horses, and fluttered like butterflies. We marched in a parade with the flag leading the way, as they played drums and bells, sticks and triangles.

I loved spending my days in that environment, with walls covered with colorful painted murals, and the air filled with music, as we marched to the melody of childhood. Children listened with wide eyed belief to stories of magic told by silly puppets. Kindergarten was a far cry from the boring, repetitive exploits of Dick and Jane. It was a whole different world, a place of exploration and creativity, finger paint and dancing, stories and play, graham crackers and comfort, music, and song. It was a unique and joyous world of laughter, fun, and best of all, in this big space, there was room to grow!

Jack and Jacky

Although Kindergarten was a joyous world, that is not to say that it remained totally untouched by tears. The first day of school was a good example. In the early sixties it was not nearly as common to send young children to pre-school. For the bulk of my students the first day of kindergarten was their first time at school. A big step, it was one that took them from the sheltered cocoon of home into an unknown world. There was a moment when I took their hand and they had to let go of mommy's. It was a traumatic one. If mom was out of sight would she return? Many times, the anxiety turned into tears. One child's tears could be contagious, another would begin to wonder if there was a reason to be truly afraid.

No doubt about it, that first day of school was a disadvantage of teaching kindergarten. But usually the tears did not last long. I would reassure them that mom would be back soon and then engage them with a game or toy. Each day the crying episodes lessened, both in number and duration, and by the second week of school they were a thing of the past. Routine was my friend. If you know snack always precedes recess and nap is always followed by story, and then mommy always appears at the classroom door, you begin to trust in the order of things.

One first day does stick in my memory. I finally had all thirty children settled and playing busily about the room. I was in the process of shooing the last parents out the door and trying to reassure one worried mom. Her son had already eagerly joined other boys at the blocks. She still remained reluctant to leave. "He'll be fine," I said.

She didn't move, her eyes brimmed with tears and before I knew it, she began crying. "I've never left him before," she said. I put my arms around her as she sobbed on my shoulder. A crying parent was a first for me in my young career. I couldn't very well distract her with a toy. Comforting her as best I could, I edged her towards the door, telling her I would see her again shortly at dismissal. She left reluctantly, sniffling and looking back over her shoulder.

Once the children settled into a routine, the class ran very smoothly. September faded into October and we carved a pumpkin at the science table and roasted the seeds to eat. The children wore their costumes to school and marched in a Halloween parade. In November we painted turkeys, a whole line of them were currently drying on the easel wall. I had to laugh at how silly they looked as I passed them on my way to the lunchroom. I brought my brown bag and sat down to chat with other teachers.

Suddenly the vice-principal's voice interrupted over the intercom. "Teachers, something is happening! We don't know the facts yet, but we are going to put our radio thru on the intercom, so you will be informed as soon as we are." We listened as an excited radio announcer babbled that there were reports that someone had fired shots at President Kennedy's motorcade in Dallas. No one knew if the president had been injured. That couldn't be true, I thought. But the next thing he said was that the motorcade was on its way to the hospital. Every minute the news changed as they learned more. The president had been wounded, no one knew how seriously. The doctors were working on him. The lunchroom atmosphere was tense with anxiety as we listened. "The trauma team will save him," I thought.

Then came the terrible announcement that no one could believe, "President Kennedy is dead." The room went silent. I looked around at all the teachers with tears sliding down their cheeks, a couple started sobbing. Everyone was shocked. I didn't want to leave, but I had less than five minutes to walk back to my room to greet my afternoon class.

At first, I didn't know what to do. Probably most of the class did not know. They had been in route for the last few minutes. Should I tell them? They were only five years old. How could they understand? I was an adult, and I couldn't understand. I thought about it. When they arrived home, they would probably be surrounded by emotional adults, perhaps unprepared to attempt an explanation. Young as they were, this was history they were living through. Someday they might remember, as I vaguely remembered the passing of Roosevelt, when I was their same age.

When they were all gathered together on the rug, I gently explained that the president of our country, Jack Kennedy, had been shot and that sadly he had died. They didn't understand dead of course, but we talked about the president and how their mommies and daddies might feel like crying. I tried to be very calm and matter of fact about the tragedy. I just had to hope that my spur of the moment decision of how to react was the right one.

School was canceled the next day and there followed the long sorrowful weekend while the entire nation grieved and clung to their televisions as history unfolded. I shed a lot of tears. I had been too young to vote in the last election, but like so many Americans, I had identified with the young family living in the White House and now I grieved with them.

When school finally resumed, there was still discussion. At sharing time one of the boys got up to excitedly inform us, "Teacher, I saw the man on the TV shoot a gun. He shotted the bad guy that killed the president!" He too had been watching the news on Sunday when Oswald was killed.

I wanted to put the tears behind us. Slowly, we resumed life as usual in kindergarten. The prevailing method when I did student teaching at the U.C.L.A.

demonstration school, was to base social studies and other learning on block play. It had not been that long since John Glenn was celebrated as a hero for orbiting the Earth in a space capsule. Many of my little boys now saw themselves as future astronauts. We decided to build a spaceship in the block area. While the children busily built the launch platform, I obtained an old voting booth for our cardboard capsule. We painted it with powdered silver tempera paint. The pointed top was covered in aluminum foil. I constructed a control panel with a light switch and hooks and old gages for the astronauts to pretend with.

In addition, I covered one long bulletin board with black butcher paper and the kids spatter painted it with white for the stars. Next, they painted the sun, planets and comets and cut them out to add to our mural. Our "space program" was very popular, especially with one shy little boy named Jacky who only liked to play with blocks.

Jacky was one of a set of twins. His twin was in another kindergarten, off in a different building. The policy was to separate twins. As sometimes happens, one twin is more dominant and larger. Jacky was the smaller one and seemed to lag behind his brother in being outgoing or trying new things, but he loved blocks. He was learning to count backwards, from ten to "blast off," perhaps before he had even mastered the usual numeric order. The twins also had another brother who was in first grade.

One Monday the teacher of the other twin came into my room upset and crying. She didn't know all the details yet but relayed what she knew of the tragic event that had happened over the weekend. Apparently, Jacky's father had taken all three boys up to a campground where he was doing some construction work. Meanwhile, the boys were playing. There was a pool there which was surrounded by a high chain link fence with locked gates. Somehow the boys found an opening and when the father looked up all three boys were in the pool. None of them knew how to swim. The father had to scale the fence before he could dive in to rescue the boys. He only managed to resuscitate two of them. The twin in the other class had drowned! After that Jacky became even more quiet and withdrawn. I felt so sad for him. He had to cope with more of a loss than most adults could handle, not only death, but the death of his twin, and he had to do it at only five years old.

My grandmother had an old superstition that "death always comes in threes." It seemed to apply to that school year, as not long after that, the kindly principal that had given me my job in kindergarten, passed away after being ill. All of the teachers shed tears as we attended the viewing together as a faculty.

Somehow loss had intruded into our happy little world. Kindergarten is normally a joyous flowering place, but, in every garden a little rain must fall. This year the tears of parents and teachers and even little children, had freely flowed. But, after the rain, the sun always comes out, to comfort with its warmth, and, to spread the brightness that lets the growth continue in our garden of kinder.

Messy Memories

Although teaching is a profession, the typical dress for it is quite different, at least at kindergarten level. The contrast with other professions, medicine for example, was very apparent. My husband Bob wore a white lab coat every day. He might have come from anatomy class smelling of formaldehyde, but the uniform was a shield from unexpected encounters with body fluids, as were his green surgical scrubs. I often wished for such protection while teaching. At times, I wondered if I should have chosen the law. I envied women who dressed for court in a silk blouse, a smart suit and high heels, an impossible outfit for kindergarten. I gazed with amazement at some of our staff. I remember looking at an upper grade teacher one day and wondering, "How can she possibly wear that?" She was dressed in a pale blue suit of the softest suede with a matching silk blouse and four-inch-high heels. I knew instantly that she did not teach kindergarten. Otherwise, her whole salary would go to her dry cleaner. I could picture the pale blue suede covered with tiny handprints of tempera paint.

When I first started teaching, I tried to dress professionally. As I adjusted to the role, I began to modify my wardrobe accordingly. I stopped wearing anything that required dry cleaning. Gone were my wool skirts and matching cashmere sweaters. No more silk blouses. I chose to wear washable skirts and shirts, often of cotton. My high heels were relegated to evening wear. I settled into comfy flat rubber soled tennis shoes, suitable for chasing an errant kid, or doing the Hokey Pokey.

Kindergarten is a messy environment. Paste and glue, starch and clay, paint and soapy water are as prevalent as oxygen. Wiping off the grimy tabletops and washing paintbrushes and paint pots is a daily chore for the teacher. The classroom sink generally resembles a Jackson Pollack.

You deal with so many substances. In the 1960s, schools were not supplied with bottles of white glue. I don't know if it hadn't been invented or was considered too expensive. Jars of paste were the adhesive we were supplied. The children applied it by digging in with their fingers and smearing it around on the paper. With all those sticky little hands, it seemed like everything in the room was soon covered with a crusty white residue of dried paste, impossible to avoid. Even later, when liquid glue replaced paste, five-year-old kids had trouble learning to use only a few drops. Making puddles of it was so much more interesting. Whenever we did papier-mache there were also puddles of liquid starch. Trails of the blue drippy substance meandered around the room.

I will never forget the first time I taught finger-painting. It was close to Valentine's Day. I put pieces of glossy finger-paint paper out on the tables for the whole class of thirty. I had never attempted this before, so I didn't know any better. I lined the tables with newspapers; it didn't seem to matter, as they moved easily aside. Next, I poured a pool of liquid starch with a glob of paint on top and let the kids dig in with both hands. They loved smearing the red paint around the paper and making valentine hearts with their fingers. Sixty little hands were immersed in red paint and liquid starch, the gooey mess oozing between their fingertips. This horrified some of the girls, which thrilled the little boys, who delighted in scaring them with "bloody" hands. They were all dressed in paint shirts or aprons, but they didn't comprehend the need to keep them on until after washing, which defeated the purpose. They had not kept the paint on the paper and the tabletops were covered with it. On the way to the sink, they touched the edges of the tables, the chairs, the faucets, the walls, and dripped on the floor. The line to use the sink was long and slow, so, why not tickle the person in front of you or pull their braids, spreading the red still further? When the day was over, the room looked like a scene out of a horror movie, a bloody disaster. Sinks and counters, tables, chairs and even the floor were smeared with red, footprints tracked paint across the floor. I attacked the scene of the disaster with soapy water and a sponge. It took me an hour after school to wash it all down, and I still had thirty paint shirts to take home and launder and my own clothes. I was unsure if I would ever do another lesson with finger-paint.

Of course, you learn from experience. An art consultant came to my class one October to lead a lesson in finger-paint. "Oh no!" I thought, but I watched her. First, she covered the tables with a roll of white butcher paper. Chairs were removed to the other side of the room. The aproned children stood around the tables as she poured little puddles of starch and paint. Each child had to keep one hand behind their back. With the other they were to smear the paint around to make a pumpkin shape and trace a face with one finger. While I wrote their names next to each pumpkin she went around and pressed their messy hand onto the paper to leave a handprint. It served to remove a lot of paint. Then they could wash their hand, return, and use a brush to paint a green pumpkin stem. After school, she removed the butcher paper, leaving a clean table, and cut out the dried pumpkins so I could display them. It was all very neat and not a drop of paint got on the carpet of that room. The next day she surprised me with a beautiful fall bouquet. She had cut out all the orange handprints, glued them onto sturdy green construction paper, cut again, added wire stems, and presented them in a vase. I would replicate that finger-paint lesson every October.

Of course, there are worse things than finger-paint. One day, the other kindergarten teacher came to my room in a panic. "Have you seen Ricky?" she asked. She was missing one little boy who had mental issues. I suggested she try the hallway restroom, as water is often an attraction. We located him hiding there. He apparently had a stomach problem, and had stripped off all his clothes, and stuffed them in the toilet in an attempt to wash them. He was now naked and covered in feces. We cleaned him up a little and dressed him in a paint shirt from my room. It was a smelly job. She escorted him to the office while I watched both classes and called the janitor to deal with the overflowing toilet.

Sometimes a child would unexpectedly throw up. Although, I got so I could usually spot the warning sign of a pale bottom lip and send them to the school nurse just in time. Otherwise, I would call the janitor and take the class outside for an unscheduled recess. However, I will never forget one day. There were ten children sitting at a long table for a craft project. I had traced the many parts needed, and each child had a neat little pile of paper pieces in front of them. I began giving careful directions on how to assemble and paste the project step by step. They were having fun, when suddenly the girl at the end of the table stood up, leaned over the table, and vomited without warning. It splattered all over the table, the cut papers and even onto the children. A couple of them began crying because their project was ruined. I had to deal with washing off hands, faces, hair and clothes while the custodian dealt with the mess on the table. Sometimes little children have no previous experience with nausea. It can take them and everyone else completely by surprise!

I often sat in a little student chair to work so I could be at their level. One day I did just that, only to realize that I had sat in a mysterious puddle. Sometimes five-year-olds are like puppies, not quite housebroken. When I stood up, my light blue denim skirt had a sopping wet dark stain down the back, embarrassing to say the least. It would have been a good idea to have a spare outfit handy in the teacher's closet, a lesson I learned. Perhaps teachers' compensation should include hazard pay.

After years of teaching, I thought I had seen it all, every possible mess. However, one day I heard a commotion on the playground just outside my door. A moment later several children ran in screaming and leading a crying boy. His head was covered with white goo dripping down his face and onto his shoulders. The front of his T-shirt was also covered with the same gunk. I was shocked to learn that the mess was courtesy of an overhead sea gull! Well, **washable** is the key word to remember in the world of kindergarten.

A Time for Slime

One Friday near the end of the school year, all kindergarten classes were scheduled for a minimum day. That meant in addition to a shortened day, all kindergarteners would attend a morning session. (I think it was for a special assembly.) Since it was a rare occurrence for us to have the afternoon free, I decided to host a luncheon for the other kindergarten teachers.

I lived in an apartment in Daly City, a short drive from the school. Although I had been there for three years, the only entertaining I had done consisted of parties for med students and their wives. (Those casual B.Y.O.B. evenings worked with our meager budget.)

Maybe it was time to bring out the newlywed presents and put them to use. I would try to give a fancy luncheon in our sparsely furnished apartment. Our dining area held only a beige metal card table and four matching folding chairs, a wedding gift from Grandma. I unwrapped a new tablecloth, and matching napkins of moss green linen, and spread it over the card table. It not only fit perfectly, but the lovely color matched the green draperies that hung at the windows, (a free recycled luxury, rescued from the Presbyterian church when they redecorated, by my mother, the pastor's secretary).

Next, the wedding china, white with a sprig of green seagrass and a silver rim. I added four place settings of sterling silver and crystal goblets with silver rims. The table looked elegant and sparkly. After school the day before the luncheon, I drove down to nearby Colma, a city with more dead residents then living ones. As a city of cemeteries, it has convenient stands that sell fresh flowers. I bought a large inexpensive bouquet of white daisies with bushy green stems. At home, I placed them in a bucket of water and put them outside on the porch for the night to keep them crisp.

Before school the next day, I quickly arranged the daisies in a vase and set them on the table. I was pleased with the perfect centerpiece and stepped back to admire the attractive table setting. Everything was ready and I hoped it would impress them.

After the early dismissal at school, I rushed to my car and drove home so I could get the salads out of the refrigerator, warm the oven for the rolls, and be ready when the other teachers arrived. I guessed I had about a half hour of lead time to work with. That was before I glanced at the table.

I stood transfixed in horror. The leafy greens of the daisies had concealed more than a dozen snails! They had obviously spent the entire morning crawling all over the table leaving evidence of that in the many silvery trails that led across the tablecloth and over the plates and silverware. My luncheon table setting was ruined! I felt like bursting into tears.

But there wasn't time to cry. I told myself, "Come on, you don't want to be a failure on your first attempt, you need to fix this, and fast." I flew into action, placing the bunch of daisies in one side of the sink and filling the other side with hot soapy water for the dishes and silver. With a damp cloth I sponged off the trail around the tablecloth. I have never washed and dried dishes so fast in my life. I reset the table and then while running cold water over the daisies, I stripped excess leaves and any remaining snails off them, something I should have done last night if I had known better. Finally, I once again popped the clean centerpiece back on the table just as the doorbell sounded. I was still blushing when I opened the door at what was almost my most embarrassing moment ever. As it was, they never knew!

I do think it's important to learn from mistakes. I learned how to more carefully prepare flowers, or better yet to buy them at a florist, instead of a cemetery. As it turns out there was another take away. The next year in kindergarten, I did a science unit on snails. We read books about them, saw a movie on snails and brought live snails into the classroom, watching them froth and slither on various surfaces.

It was the resulting creative art activity that I found the most satisfying. One day I placed pieces of dark brown construction paper on the table and then, remembering my luncheon, we placed more than a dozen snails onto the papers and observed them as they slowly meandered around the table leaving a path of glistening slime behind them. When the papers were dry the children were fascinated that if they looked closely, they could still see the silvery residue where the snails had traveled.

That gave me an idea. I mixed up some metallic silver tempera paint and gave each child a small watercolor brush. They slowly and carefully traced the pathways with silver paint. When trimmed and mounted together the pieces of paper made an artistic bulletin board. An intricate pattern of shining lines looped across the dark brown background forming a delicate design engraved in elegant silver. With cut out letters I captioned the bulletin board: SNAIL TRAILS.

Not long after that luncheon I left my job in So. San Francisco. After three years in that kindergarten room, I was sad to leave, but it left a trail of memories behind that still shine like silver.

Paula

When my husband graduated from medical school, we moved back to Southern California for his internship at USC County Hospital. Our new apartment was in Alhambra, two blocks from where I lived as a child. I obtained a teaching job with Alhambra City Schools. The new job brought two big rewards into my life: a new kindergarten room and a forever friend. The second came about because of my choice of the first.

I had been offered contracts by both Pasadena and Alhambra school districts. I accepted Alhambra because they showed me a beautiful kindergarten room, promising it to me should I sign with them. Modern with lots of blonde wood, it was long with a stage at one end, as though it had been a theater room. All but the stage was covered with new avocado green carpeting.

The teacher was retiring. However, during the summer that teacher changed her mind and wanted to return to her room. The district called me and said they would honor their promise if I wanted; but to accommodate her they had an alternative to offer.

I was disappointed, but went to view the room at Ramona School, prepared to dislike it. When I walked in, I was surprised. The room was old, but it was huge. In fact, it was the largest room in the school. Upon entering, the first thing you saw was a real fireplace, set at an angle, with a wood mantle and a spacious hearth. It was made of historic old Pasadena ceramic tiles, green and maroon. It probably once held a gas flame stove that had since been removed. Although it no longer functioned, I could imagine filling it with picture books with cushions on the hearth for children to sit and read. Perhaps there could be paper Christmas stockings displayed from the mantle. Along the left wall there was a long alcove with low shelves, perfect for a science center. The front of the room held an area rug for the children to sit on and an upright piano of dark wood. The ceilings were high and the wall to my right was all windows. The huge room continued back with banks of built-in cabinets painted a soothing grey green. At the far end of the room were double doors that exited to the side street. If you turned left, the L-shaped room continued. It held a bank of built-in easels and a wall of hooks to hold paint shirts. At the end of the L were two restrooms. Off of that art area was another small room, a kitchen/ teacher work room with a sink and a kiln oven for firing clay.

The decision was an easy one. Although the room was not carpeted it was gigantic with wonderful space and storage and I also wouldn't have to feel guilty about depriving another teacher of her room. The old two-story stone building was historic. I later found out that my father had attended kindergarten in that same room.

One afternoon as I was fixing up my room, the door to the hall opened and the principal brought in a brunette girl, introducing her as the other new kindergarten teacher. She had just graduated from Whittier College and this would be her first teaching assignment. Little did we know that would be the beginning of a friendship that would last for fifty years.

Paula occupied a small former first-grade room across the hall from mine. Since this would be my fifth year of teaching, she constantly turned to me for ideas. (I had also been given a wealth of material by my mother-in-law who had taught kindergarten for over thirty years.) I was glad to share: fingerplays, poems, flannel board stories, and arts and crafts projects.

We formed an instant friendship. As my room was large and hers so small, we often combined our classes. My room could easily accommodate our sixty to seventy children at the tables for an art activity. I would demonstrate the project for both classes, and Paula provided extra helping hands for the children. We also often joined both kindergartens together for music time. Paula was a more accomplished piano player and I had just taken up guitar, so we complemented each other. Years later, team teaching became a popular concept, but we began doing it because we enjoyed working together, and the children benefited from two teachers.

We would also take both classes to the playground together for recess. It gave us a chance to chat while they were playing. At first this annoyed the principal, but Paula convinced him that she needed a restroom break and this was a convenient solution.

One day, getting the classes together almost got us in trouble. The district had a curriculum supervisor who would drop in unexpectedly and observe and report her suggestions to the principal and the district. On the day she arrived in my class, I was demonstrating making a fire engine from construction paper to both classes. She watched and then left the room with a frown on her face. Later in the afternoon, on the spur of the moment, I invited Paula's class over to share a movie on the fire department, because it gave us the opportunity to sit and whisper. Suddenly, back came the supervisor. She stayed only a moment and left. I thought, "Oops." After school she returned unexpectedly full of nothing but compliments. She admitted that she had been critical of my doing a fire engine art activity without an accompanying social studies lesson, but was thrilled to find out that it was because I was planning to show the movie later. I was happy to let her think that had really been my strategy as she wrote up her evaluation.

For the next three years Paula and I did everything together. There was an hour and a half break between morning and afternoon class sessions. We often went out to lunch. There were several places close by. Sometimes it would be hamburgers at Bob's Big Boy, or hot pastrami at The Hat, or our favorite, a drive-in called Toohey's, where we would both order a number two burger with pickles and onions and the carhop would place a tray on the window of my car.

Sometimes the timing was tight, especially when the weather got warm. The minute the morning class was out the door, we would hop into my sportscar, a shiny black Jaguar XKE. With the top down, we would zip to the taco stand on Valley Boulevard. Equipped with two tacos and cokes we would rush to my nearby apartment, don our bikinis, lunch by my pool, and enjoy a refreshing swim. Then, with our wet hair drying in the breeze, the Jag would roar up to the school. We hurried, but sometimes the principal would be standing by the gate waiting and glowering at his watch. But we were always careful to get back with a minute or two to spare. Sometimes our constant togetherness annoyed him, but fortunately I think we were also his favorite teachers.

One morning, I was pulling up to the side of the school in my XKE. I slowed in preparation to turn into a driveway, so I could turn around and park. An impatient driver came around the corner behind me and must have thought I was slowing to drop off a kid on my right. He was in a hurry and decided to go around me. Just as I began my left turn into a driveway, he floored it and hit my Jag broadside, crumpling the long hood. He then bounced off my car and careened into Paula's parked brand new red Chevy Camaro, the rosy apple of her eye. It smashed the front of her car too.

Fortunately, no one was injured. A concerned parent rushed down to the office to report the accident and tell them to call the police. "The kindergarten teacher's car has been in an accident!" she announced excitedly.

"Which kindergarten teacher's car?" the secretary asked.

"Both of them!" she exclaimed.

At which point the principal quipped, "You might know they wouldn't do anything separately!"

Me Turning the Jump Rope on the Ramona Playground

Kelli

One student stands out in my memory from my first year at Ramona. I noticed Kelli right away as she was one of the first to follow directions and be eager to participate. She always sat quietly at story time and was very attentive during lessons, a joy for any teacher. She quickly became one of my favorite students.

Something unique about Kelli was her hair. You couldn't help but notice it. It was long and thick, reaching almost to her waist. Every day it was fixed in a different hairstyle. Sometimes brushed in waves, other times braided in French braids or pigtails tied with colorful ribbons. There were beautiful long sausage curls or fancy updos topped with an elaborate bow. The variety was endless. She was also always dressed very nicely in freshly laundered little dresses and shining shoes. It was obvious someone lavished a lot of care and attention on Kelli.

At parent/teacher conferences held in November, I met with Kelli's mom. She was a very friendly lady, and I told her how well Kelli was doing in school and that I enjoyed having her in class. I also complimented her on how she fixed Kelli's hair. "Oh, I used to work as a hairdresser," she said, "but now I am a stay-at-home mom since Kelli was born. I just do her hair now." She mentioned that to earn a little extra money she also babysat her neighbor's toddler.

That was the moment that gave me an idea. "Now that Kelli is in school, would you be interested in taking care of another toddler?" I asked. Since September a woman in the apartment house next to ours had been babysitting my three-year-old son and I had been increasingly dissatisfied. He only had a small living room area to play in. When

I would arrive to pick him up in the afternoons, he would be sitting on the floor with a toy while she lazily watched television in the darkened room with all the blinds pulled down. It was not a very stimulating environment. I was seeking a change. The resulting new arrangement was positive for everyone. It solved my babysitting problem and provided extra income for Kelli's mom. Kelli's family lived in a nice little house a couple blocks from the school. It had a back yard and a lawn with lots of wheel toys for playtime. Lunch and nutritious snacks were provided, and there was a quiet room for naptime. When I would pick my son up in the afternoons he was usually playing with Kelli. Her mom took wonderful care of Jeff for the rest of the years I worked at Ramona, even after he began attending kindergarten in Paula's afternoon class.

It was interesting that a convenient childcare solution came about through teaching, a career choice that facilitates a working mom. The result was like one of Kelli's elaborate hairdos, perfect and tied up with a bow on top!

The Principal

When I started teaching, the position of school principal was generally held by a man, usually assisted by a vice principal. In South San Francisco, the only principal I had worked for had been a kind older man who gave me my first kindergarten job. He passed away while I taught there. Moving to a new school meant getting a new principal.

Ramona was an old traditional school, built of stone and brick with steps leading up to the impressive front entrance. I was not surprised when I met the principal for the first time. He too was old and impressive. With silver hair, he was wearing a dark suit, a tie, and a dignified stony expression.

After I started work there, I began to learn more about him. Mr. D. ran a tight ship. He held very few faculty meetings, seeming to consider group input a waste of time. He made it clear what the rules were, and that he expected the staff to follow them. The school functioned well. He never scheduled lesson observations, but would unexpectedly pop into my room, slowly walk around for a couple minutes and then leave without comment. It was a bit intimidating. I guessed he would let me know if he had anything negative to say, but he maintained an enigmatic silence.

He kept a sharp eye on the budget. One of his pet peeves was the cost of supplies. He did not permit an open supply room. Instead, at the beginning of each month, teachers turned in a written list of material requests. The list would be returned, either with the supplies, or with red lines drawn through any items he felt were unnecessary. Unfortunately, kindergarten required more supplies than other grades. Because, at that time we taught two class sessions. Also, instead of using textbooks, we did daily art or craft projects.

One December, the second year I was there, Mr. D. was on a money saving campaign and everyone's supply requests were being significantly cut back. My December list came back slashed through with red pencil lines, eliminating many of the supplies I needed. Other teachers, in the same situation, angrily complained to Mr. D., only to be met with firm denials. I decided to adopt a different tactic.

I carefully made up an example of an intended craft project, a giant Santa face of construction paper fitted around a wire coat hanger. The hat concealed the hook. He had a red nose, rosy cheeks, and a long white beard that the children could fringe and curl. I took the completed creation and marched down to the principal's office. "Mr. D.," I said cheerily as I approached, "I brought you a present to decorate your office door! Isn't he cute?" I asked.

"Well, er thank you" he said.

"The kindergarten parents love getting these," I said, playing my best card. "They like to decorate for the holidays with their child's schoolwork."

"Very nice," he said with a ghost of a smile.

"The problem is I don't have enough supplies for each child to make one." I stated, as I whipped out my red-penciled list. "You see, he requires one piece of red paper for his hat and one of peach for his face and one white for the beard. I have two classes of 35 students, so I need 70 pieces of each paper color. There are only 50 sheets in a packet of construction paper. I need the two packages of each that I requested, so each student can make one." I laid my supply request in front of him where he could plainly see all the twos that were crossed out and changed to ones. "I only asked for what I needed," I said calmly.

He looked at me for a minute then cleared his throat and said, "Well, yes, I can see that." He barked impatiently, "I'll fill the rest of your order." The Santa face looked very festive on the principal's office door for the rest of the month. From then on, my supply requests usually came back with no red lines.

In another supply related incident, Mr. D. stormed into my room one day while I was in the middle of reading a story. "Where do you store your colored paper?" he demanded with a red face. I pointed to the correct cupboard and he crossed over to it, jerked open the tall door and stood quietly glaring. He stared at the contents for a couple minutes with a stern look on his face. Then he closed the cabinet and walked out of my room without a word of explanation. I later learned that he had been on a tear to prevent waste, going through each classroom to check on how paper was stored. He had become enraged in some classes where he found paper jammed into piles causing it to rip or wrinkle.

Did I mention that my lovely kindergarten room had a wall of built-in wood cabinets? One of which was fitted from bottom to top with shelves for paper every two inches, perfect for storing a different color on each shelf. Being more than a bit compulsive, I would always take the cellophane off a new package and line up the edges of the new sheets perfectly with the old ones. Not only that, but I also color coded the shelves of paper so that they advanced neatly in order from warm to cool colors. That is what Mr. D. saw when he opened the cabinet, but he never mentioned a word about it.

It was in my third year at Ramona that the principal called me into his office to tell me that California State College at Los Angeles wished to place two student teachers at our school, and he had decided to put one in each kindergarten. I had never been a master teacher before, but this sounded good to me, not that he was asking my permission. Imagine my surprise when the student teacher turned out to be my first cousin, Sharon. She had put in a request to be assigned to my class. Her best friend was assigned to the other kindergarten, which was taught by Paula, my best friend. I was surprised that Mr. D. had agreed to it.

Having a student teacher turned out to be very helpful, as I had so many students. There are lots of times with little ones that you wish you had an extra set of hands; my wish came true. A student teacher cut the ratio of children to adults in half. Also, Sharon was on her second student teaching assignment and was very comfortable and competent with the children. We had grown up together, so working together was just natural. At that time, adult help in the classroom was rare; there were no paid aides and parent volunteers were not allowed. It was great to finish out the first semester with a student teacher. When the semester ended, Sharon and her friend, having earned their teaching credentials, were seeking employment.

Meanwhile the state legislature passed a law that made a dramatic change in the structure of kindergarten. Ever since I began teaching, kindergarten teachers, as opposed to other grades, had to teach two class sessions each day. Each consisted of a duration of two hours and thirty minutes. (According to my mother-in-law, who had taught kindergarten for thirty-five years, it had always been like that.) The new law would extend the kindergarten day to three hours and twenty minutes, requiring a separate teacher for each session.

This was a huge change. I had currently been teaching two classes of thirty-five students each. That required seventy parent conferences and report cards and seventy daily art projects to prepare, etc. This would cut my workload in half. It also created two job openings at our school. Mr. D. hired my cousin and her friend as the new kindergarten teachers. Sharon and I, who had shared our childhood, were now sharing a classroom, each teaching a session. As far as we were concerned this law couldn't have come at a more perfect time. We enjoyed working together as we had enjoyed playing together as children. I was grateful to Mr. D. for allowing it.

Dramatic changes in my personal life were also taking place. My husband and I had separated. As the school year drew to a close, I reluctantly decided to move to the beach for a fresh start. My friend Paula was also moving. We both left Ramona, as did Mr. D. who retired at the same time.

When Sharon and I were growing up, we had celebrated holidays together and were often given identical gifts, including matching dresses and "twin" outfits. Sharon was two years younger and had often inherited my outgrown clothing. Unexpectedly, funding for the new law expired, so in September, kindergartens would return to the old schedule in one room. It seemed strange that now my cousin would also inherit both my job and my beautiful classroom. (As it turned out, twenty-five-year-old Sharon would continue to teach at Ramona until she turned seventy.)

I applied to two school districts at the beach, Fountain Valley and Newport-Mesa. My preference was Newport-Mesa, but it was more difficult to get an interview with and was hiring less. During my appointment at Fountain Valley the personnel director read over my application. He looked at me oddly and asked, "What was your principal like; was he a young man?"

I thought that was a strange question, but I answered, "No, I believe he was in his mid-sixties, in fact he just retired. The whole staff was a little scared of him, but he ran the school very efficiently."

"Well," he said, "I just asked because I have to tell you that in all my years as personnel director, I have never read such a flattering recommendation letter." I was shocked! Mr. D. didn't do compliments. I never did get to read the letter, but it was apparently effective. I received contract offers from both districts. Perhaps I owed my new job in Newport-Mesa to the principal who used to walk so unexpectedly through my classroom, without a smile or a comment, always silent. But, how like him to finally have the last word.

Change

Sometimes a year in life comes along that is packed full of changes. After leaving Alhambra, I moved to an apartment in Costa Mesa. It was freshly painted white, with brand new carpet. I planted pots of pink geraniums on the balcony that overlooked vacant fields behind a boat building yard. I couldn't see the ocean, but I could smell the sea air. I was fulfilling my dream of living at the beach. I spent the summer dating, sunning on the sand, and waiting for my divorce to become final.

I had only myself to rely on now, if my car refused to start, I would have no way to get to school. I needed another change. I sold my temperamental used Jaguar and purchased a reliable new Mustang.

In the fall, I began my new teaching job at Bear Street School in Costa Mesa. The kindergarten classroom was a big change from the one in Alhambra. That had been a huge room in an historic old school. This school was only two years old, and the classroom much smaller. Built as a kindergarten room, it did contain restrooms and a wall of built-in paint easels. Attached to the room was a workroom and a teacher restroom. It had some compensating advantages over my former room: new wall-to-wall carpeting, sliding glass doors to an outdoor patio, and an attached kindergarten playground. I no longer had to line children up and walk them along a hall and downstairs to get them to recess. This was more convenient.

I did encounter a problem. Bear Street school was so small that it did not have a first or second grade, so my six-year-old son could not attend there. He would have to go to a school close to our apartment and I would need to employ a sitter for after school care. I didn't know what to do until I attended the reception for new teachers. I began chatting with the district personnel director and explained my dilemma.

"I can take care of that," he said and went on to explain his solution. Jeff would be allowed an intra-district permit to attend at nearby Paularino School which was handling the first graders for Bear Street. I could drop Jeff off at his school on my way to work in the morning, and after school he would be bussed over to my school, arriving fifteen minutes after I dismissed my class. I was amazed at the convenient solution.

"Don't worry," the personnel director said. "In this district we take care of our own!" That proved true. I was grateful to not need a sitter. The schedule worked perfectly. Jeff arrived in my classroom each day just in time to be my little helper. We followed that plan for the first year I taught there, and the next year Bear Street incorporated a second-grade class.

Meanwhile, the law that had established a longer kindergarten day had expired and the state reverted to the old system. Once again, I was teaching both a morning and an afternoon session. I settled back into the old schedule.

An even bigger change occurred in my personal life. I had continued to date a boyfriend from Alhambra after my move. I thought, "If he really loves me, he won't let an hour's drive stop him," and he didn't. We got married over Christmas vacation.

In January I was in the middle of teaching when my principal walked into my classroom with news of another change. The state legislature had reinstated the kindergarten extended day law. I would be teaching only one session for the rest of the year and a new teacher would be hired for the other. He proceeded to introduce me to Darlene, the smiling lady standing next to him. I chose to keep the afternoon class and she took over the morning group. This was an enormous change. In every other grade a teacher's classroom is her own little world that belongs solely to her. But kindergarten is unique. In the future I would be sharing everything with another teacher: the classroom, the children, the planning, and team teaching. Would it work?

The new kindergarten day expanded from two and a half hours long to three hours and twenty minutes. There was no set direction given for what to do with the extra fifty minutes. It was intended that there would be more academic readiness included, so I came up with an idea. I called it Workshop. There was a bank of cupboards at floor level all along one wall, divided into cubby holes. During the fifty minutes of Workshop, I would open the cupboard doors and the children could choose an item from a cubby. They contained word puzzles, alphabet games, math manipulatives, sound matching games etc., all designed to teach some beginning academic concept. The kids would sit on the cozy carpeted floor in pairs and work together. Meanwhile a small group also worked with Darlene or me with such things as writing alphabet letters or playing math Bingo. This was a big shift in the philosophy of kindergarten, which had been focused on social adjustment and creative play as the "work" of kindergarten. It was the beginning of change in the direction of a more academic curriculum.

Meanwhile, it did not prove to be as painful as I expected to give up half of my classroom bespace. When I lived in small apartments, my kindergarten room had felt like an addition to my home, extra space to store things, an added benefit of teaching. Although I now had to share my schoolroom, after two months of marriage, my husband and I had bought a house. So, I had added a lot of available storage space in a rambling fixer upper in Newport Beach.

It is difficult to know whether changes will prove beneficial. I was emerging from the cocoon of the familiar into the unknown. What would be the results of that metamorphosis?

With the perspective that comes with years, I can look back with answers. My move to the beach was a wonderful decision. I love it here. My Christmas wedding was the beginning of a forty-seven-year happy marriage. Jeff's year at Paularino gave him a male teacher whose specialty was reading, and Jeff quickly became the most advanced reader in the class. He couldn't have had a better start, becoming a lifetime A student. Meeting Darlene was the beginning of a close friendship that lasted for three decades. We enjoyed remodeling the fixer upper house for the next thirty-two years. The lengthened day schedule in kindergarten remained a permanent change and marked the beginning of an increase in the content of instruction. It resulted in a more academic and beneficial curriculum. In retrospect, I think perhaps that metamorphosis released a butterfly. It emerged into golden sunlight and fluttered upwards on the wings of change.

A Treetop View

I began my new job at Bear Street School in 1968. It was very different from the old traditional school I had just left. This was a new building constructed in an innovative circular design with classrooms surrounding a central pod workroom. It faced Bear Street, a quiet two-lane road with little traffic. It was located in a mostly agricultural area, next to a large lima bean field with a green clapboard farmhouse standing in front. In fact, one of my students lived there. I remember one afternoon walking next door through the bean field for a parent conference.

Some of the adjacent fields had been used to establish a new shopping center called South Coast Plaza. It had opened a year earlier in March of 1967 and contained two big anchor stores, May Co. and Sears. It constantly had construction going on as it continued to grow.

My classroom was on the other side of the school, on the corner of Bear Street and Paularino Street. The kindergarten playground adjoined a vacant lot on Paularino, bordered by a row of tall Eucalyptus trees. I loved doing yard duty in that setting. On warm days I would leave my classroom door open so I could enjoy the view. As I sat reading at story time, I could gaze out and see sheep contentedly grazing. It was calm and peaceful.

During the next five years, the view began to change. There was gradually more traffic going by my corner. The shopping center continued to grow as it gobbled up the bean fields. Houses were built nearby where strawberries once grew. Gone were the grazing sheep. One day, I learned that the giant Eucalyptus trees were scheduled to be cut down, in preparation for the widening of Paularino street. I was sad that the row of magnificent trees would soon be destroyed.

I watched from my classroom as city trucks and tree trimmers arrived to start work. I decided this would be an educational opportunity for the children to observe the workmen. I took the class outside and lined them up next to the short chain link fence that divided our playground from the vacant lot. We had a front row seat to the interesting action.

We watched as lower branches were cut off and fed into a machine that chewed them up. This seemed to fascinate the kids. Next, a man in a cage extension on top of a truck, was lifted high up to one of the huge trees. He affixed a heavy rope around the top of the tree. Then he was lowered about halfway down the tree and used a chain saw to partially cut through the thick trunk. I could see they intended to have the top of the tree fall lengthwise on the field by pulling on the rope with the truck. But even should it fall in our direction, we were a safe distance away as the lot was so wide.

Next, the man who had made the cut in the tree was lowered down to the ground. The truck slowly backed up the length of the field, gradually tightening the heavy rope. The other workmen and vehicles retreated to the far corner of the lot. Gradually the rope grew taught as the truck continued to reverse. The children and I watched in excited anticipation of the dramatic moment when the treetop would break away. The truck continued to back up and pull. The tension increased. I wondered if the rope would hold. The tree bent and then, with a loud crack, the partially severed trunk gave way.

"Ohhh!" Thirty little mouths called out a gasping exclamation at the noise. The truck continued to tug, but the top of the tree did not instantly fall. A part of the trunk still held. The treetop swayed wildly and then, in what seemed like slow motion, it spun around in a circular movement before falling with a loud crash.

Despite the pull of the guiding rope, the tree did not fall in the intended direction. Instead, it spiraled and fell toward the street. Unfortunately, it landed with a tremendous crash directly on a passing car. The entire front of the car was completely crushed under the huge tree. The windshield was shattered in a sickening circular pattern where the driver's head had struck. The driver himself was just visible, slumped unconscious, or worse, over the steering wheel. For a moment I stood there staring in silent shock at the unexpected result, unable to believe what I had just seen.

Then I noticed all the little faces looking up at me, waiting to see my reaction. I snapped back into teacher mode, "Alright everyone, get in line now. We are going back inside." Fortunately, they obediently did as they were told.

This was before cell phones and I didn't know if anyone in the houses facing the streets had been home to see or call the police. Back inside, I immediately picked up my classroom phone and called the office. "There has been a bad accident on the street outside my room. Please call the police and report it. They need to send an ambulance right away!"

I gathered the children together. We talked about what we had seen. I told them that the tree didn't fall where it was supposed to and that landing on top of the car was an accident. "The car got smashed!" one of the boys blurted out.

"Did the man get killed?" another asked.

"No, Bobby," I said optimistically. "He was hurt but an ambulance is taking him to the hospital so he can get better." I certainly was hoping that was the case. I hoped I had not unintentionally traumatized these little ones by having them observe a fatality occurring. I tried to be calm and matter of fact and reassure them. They seemed to take their cue from my behavior and although there were questions, there were no tears.

The following day the newspaper account of the accident mentioned only that the man was in the hospital being treated for his injuries. I heard nothing further for a long while.

At the time, my husband worked as a director for the City of Newport Beach. Through him we had become acquainted with a very nice young couple. The husband was a lawyer who handled legal work for cities. One night when we were out to dinner with them, he mentioned he was defending a city in a case where a tree had fallen on a passing motorist.

What a co-incidence. I mentioned that I thought I was the first to call in about the accident. I asked how the man was now. He said that he had been unconscious but had completely recovered. He was now suing the city of Cost Mesa for damages. His car had been totaled in addition to medical bills and trauma. City workers said they had tried to stop the car. The driver claimed the street had not been blocked off and he had never been warned to stop. Our lawyer friend got excited when I said I was standing there with my class watching the whole incident.

"Would you be willing to be a witness in court?" he asked. "What did you see the workers doing? Were they stopping cars?"

Unfortunately, I had to admit that I would be useless as a witness. My whole focus had been centered on the tree. I had not paid any attention to what had been going on at the street corner. I never did find out the final disposition of the case. Probably the city settled and the settlement was kept confidential. I was just relieved to learn that the man had survived.

In retrospect it was a memorable teaching day. When I took the class out to watch, I had in mind that the experience would be educational. In a way, for me, it was. I learned that what you expect to see is not necessarily what does unfold. I had been standing in a location with a clear view, but my perception was not complete. I failed to observe the periphery, the corner where life-changing actions were simultaneously occurring. It made me stop and think. I wonder how often I miss seeing the big picture right in front of me? How often am I only focused on a detail that I perceive to be important, when I may have just a narrow treetop view.

At Bear St. school my little corner classroom was a center court seat from which to observe a maelstrom of change. The bean fields had begun their transition into a world-famous shopping mall. The bucolic scene around me was disappearing and becoming unrecognizable, giving way to rampant progress. Outside my quiet kindergarten, the world was transforming dramatically. I'm not sure how much of that bigger picture I had even noticed. Perhaps because I focused only on the sheep at story time.

Bear Street Playground

Ready or Not

To register for kindergarten, a child had to turn five years of age on or before the second of December. This made for a very wide range of readiness for learning within a class. There were four-year-olds with birthdays in November, side by side with children who would turn six in December. Needless to say, they possessed very different abilities and learning needs. Small muscle co-ordination matured a little slower for boys than for girls. Almost every class had a couple boys with fall birthdays who presented an extra challenge. They required extra help with pencils, crayons, and especially scissors, not knowing how to hold them. They had sometimes not been allowed to use them.

Robin was a typical November boy. He exhibited all the usual four-year-old behaviors. He talked non-stop and constantly asked, "Why?" but rarely listened to the answer. Small motor activities were difficult for him. When he tried to copy letters, the effort was slow and laborious. His letters turned out looking like a shaky row of snails. The school activities he enjoyed were block play and outdoor activities at recess, mostly riding the large tricycles. He was completely unable to sit still in one place, even for a few minutes, especially if he had to be quiet. He was cheerful and energetic, seeming to bounce from one activity to another. Like many November boys, he would have been more appropriately placed in a year of pre-school. That was often not a realistic choice for parents, due to economic reasons. Most pre-schools were private and costly, while public school provided welcome free babysitting.

Robin typically had a lot of difficulty settling down to any sort of game or readiness activity. Not only was writing or coloring a chore, but scissors were an impossibility. His eye-hand co-ordination and interest was just not there yet. A floor puzzle was an opportunity to crawl around on the rug, which he liked to do with regularity. In fact, he often reminded me of a roly poly, one of those little bugs I used to collect as a child. They had a lot of wiggly legs, and when touched, they would curl up tight into a compact ball. I would hide them in my pockets to surprise my mom when she did the laundry.

Robin liked to roll around on the rug and had to be coaxed to come for story reading, which followed nap time. One day I looked up to see that the children had finished folding their rest mats and had come to the circle. All except Robin that is. Like a roly poly, he was curled in a ball on his mat, sound asleep. He had his thumb in his mouth and his forefinger rested on his nose. His chubby rosy cheeks worked as if he were enjoying a bedtime bottle. It was a touching sight. I was reminded how close to babyhood kindergartners really are. I said, "Shhhh," to the other children and read the story, softly, so as not to disturb the sleeper.

Robin usually verbally rambled on at sharing time. One Monday was no different, as he talked about the weekend. "My daddy went riding on a dune buggy in Mexico. He went up and down a big hill of sand and the buggy turned upside down and my dad fell out!" He was a little breathless, as if he knew this was exciting news.

"Oh no," I responded, "Did your dad get hurt?" I asked.

He seemed confused by the question. "His neck got broked," he said calmly.

I thought I was hearing an exaggeration, a result of four-year-old imagination. "Did Daddy go to the hospital?" I probed.

"No," he said in a matter-of-fact voice. "He's just dead." End of story, end of sharing.

I was confused. The story was so bizarre that I went to check at the office after school. By then, someone from his home had called in to inform us that Robin's dad had indeed been killed over the weekend, in a dune buggy accident in Mexico! Obviously, Robin had no idea yet of what that really meant. He would continue to wonder when his father might get back from Mexico.

He was not alone in experiencing tragedy that year. A girl named Susie stood up for sharing one morning and made an equally shocking announcement. "My brother got knocked off his bike by a car," she said in a matter-of-fact tone.

"Oh no! Is he alright?" I questioned.

"Well, he's dead," she said. Again, I questioned if what I was hearing was fact. I wondered why she would be in school in the immediate wake of such a tragedy. But then she said, "A lot of people are at my house, and everyone is crying a whole lot." That had the ring of truth. Probably they wanted to get her away from that for a while.

Later I found out that her nine-year-old brother had been riding his bike in the field behind the school and had ridden out on to Paularino street, right in front of a car. The teen-aged driver's view had been obstructed by the block wall at the edge of the field and by a parked car.

Susie was a spring birthday, taller and filled with bubbly confidence. She had better co-ordination than Robin. Those few months difference in age make a big difference in academic readiness. But like in most children their age, there was no readiness to begin to absorb the concept of death. Some children may have experienced the death of a beloved pet. They may see firsthand that their hamster can no longer move, or know that Rover is not around anymore, but the idea of the permanence of death doesn't seem to be there. Perhaps that is a built-in protection for young children. Susie seemed puzzled by all the family tears. Robin became less rambunctious. Both were more subdued.

On one sunny day, the entire school gathered on the lawn in front of the school. We watched as a tree was planted for Susie's brother and a bronze plaque was placed next to the sapling as a permanent memorial. It was a way to provide comfort for his young classmates and his sister Susie; they would remember him as they watched the little tree continue to grow.

I think Robin moved away at the end of that school year. I have kept a present he gave me at Christmas. It is an ornament in the shape of a little green elf wearing a pointed hat. It has a chubby face, as round as a roly poly. Each year when I hang it on my holiday tree, I am reminded of Robin.

I recall that year, when I tried to be of comfort to those little ones, ready to listen, attempting to keep their school world as normal and reassuring as possible. It was the year I learned that the kindergarten age child does not yet have any concept of the significance of death. Although each child is unique in readiness for school, no one is ever ready to learn about the sorrow that accompanies loss. Kindergarten is way too soon. There is no set age when the harsh reality of death becomes part of our lives. It arrives without warning. It does not announce itself, saying as children do when playing Hide and Seek, "Ready or not, here I come!"

Of Mice and Kids

One good thing about being a kindergarten teacher is that you are never bored. Every day is unique. You can never accurately predict what might happen next. On one memorable day, the principal was scheduled to visit my classroom. As if that was not enough, he wasn't coming alone. He was bringing the district superintendent and a couple members of the school board. I guess I should have been flattered that the principal had chosen my classroom for a visitation. However, it meant he would expect us to be doing an activity worth showing off. A scheduled observation makes even the most experienced teacher feel a bit apprehensive. You want to have everything running smoothly and to demonstrate complete control. The problem is that you are working with people, in this case, very little people. Children constitute a variable that is highly unpredictable, somewhat like an unstable substance in chemistry. You cannot possibly anticipate everything that might come up or guess the impact of an unforeseen event. I have learned to expect the unexpected.

On this particular day, I was as prepared as I could possibly be. The classroom looked neat and attractive, showcasing colorful bulletin boards. My lesson plans were displayed on my desk. The materials for the day's activities were set out in careful readiness for a good day in kindergarten. The time for the visitors' arrival was approaching. Some of the children were enjoying a craft project at the table. A few were occupied with learning games or puzzles on the rug. Others were busy at the writing center or getting ready to paint at the easels. A few were in the playhouse or observing things at the science center. A final group was at a table with the aide, preparing to make applesauce. She was helping them to peel and slice apples and placing the slices in a large kettle simmering on a hot plate. Everything was humming along perfectly, just the way it should be!

I was supervising the many moving parts but found myself a bit distracted watching the clock and waiting for our important visitors. I wasn't exactly in the mood for interruptions; but, of course, five-year-old are all about interruptions. One of the children from the art area came over, tapped me on the leg and said, "Teacher, there are eyes in the paint shirt box."

I wasn't sure I had heard him correctly. "What?" I asked.

"There are eyes in the paint shirt box!" he repeated in a louder voice. His own eyes looked enormous, like he had just seen an alien from outer space. Kindergartners are relentlessly persistent with what they want to tell the teacher, so, you might as well pay attention the first time. Patiently, I went over to investigate the paint shirt box. A little of his fear must have been contagious. I cautiously removed the shirts, one by one, and peered down into the shadowy depths of the tall box. Sure enough, all I could see in the dark bottom were two glittering *eyes!* They were staring right back at me.

One of the best things about five-year-olds is their imagination. They have a boundless capacity to believe or make up all sorts of things. I had just time to think, well, for once, it's the truth! Then a voice rang out from the science center. "Mrs. Munson, Stevie let the mouse out of the cage!"

The comment registered just as one of the other children helpfully tipped over the paint shirt box saying, "I'll catch him!" Just that fast, the mouse was out of the box and running! Little girls began screaming! Little boys began chasing the mouse to every corner of the room! My cries for order went unheard amid the excitement and general din. The mouse ran to the playhouse, followed closely by thirty frantic five–year-olds.

He moved incredibly fast! Even sixty little hands could not corral him. He managed to escape through the doorway leading to the teacher workroom.

The children knew better than to go in there. I managed to quickly shush the class a little and turned them over to the aide. I grabbed a broom and a shoebox and followed, hot on the trail of the mouse.

Now the school was designed in a pod, several classrooms opening off the central workroom. I entered the workroom in time to see a skinny tail disappear into the third-grade classroom. I peered around the door cautiously. The teacher was in front of the room with her back to me, lecturing to an attentive class. She too was undoubtedly expecting visitors, but not us, and certainly not a mouse. In subsequent years, this teacher would become an important supervisor in the district, but even then, she dressed the part. She looked proper and professional in a conservative suit and high heels. I had no way of knowing about her phobia of mice! I tried to slip in quietly, "Excuse me," I apologized, "I just need to catch our white mouse."

The words I would normally use to describe this teacher are, efficient, sophisticated and in control. None of these seemed an appropriate description for the screaming lady with the wild look on her face who had, despite her high heels, managed to jump on top of a third-grader's desk. She was doing a good balancing act up there while frantically shouting, "Catch it!" With the help of the excited third graders who were also shouting, I managed to use the broom to corral the mouse into the shoebox. I popped the lid on and apologized to a pale and shaken teacher as I exited her classroom, leaving behind a wake of total chaos.

I quickly returned to my room and replaced the wandering mouse in its cage. The children were all excitedly talking at once; the noise level was at an all-time high. I looked around the classroom. Paint was spilled, shirts were scattered across the carpet. Everything was overturned, in complete disarray from the recent chase. The playhouse particularly was a shamble. Meanwhile, the aide had been so distracted she had forgotten to stir the huge kettle of applesauce. It was now busily boiling over onto the hot plate. The smell of scorched sugar filled our room. As the door opened to admit the Superintendent and the school board visitors, I heard my principal's booming voice ring out, "**and this is our kindergarten!**"

Kevin

From the time she was a junior in high school, my daughter, Dana, also wanted to be a kindergarten teacher. I think it was not only due to my influence, but the fact that my best friends were all teachers. So was my cousin and one of my sisters. While growing up Dana was surrounded by teachers. Often, she listened to them recounting their classroom stories. It was not surprising that teaching eventually became her career goal.

During high school she obtained a summer job at our church as a day camp counselor. She worked with elementary age children teaching music and art and leading recreation for several summers.

After graduating from high school, she enrolled in local Orange Coast College and began taking classes toward an Associate of Arts degree. One of her classes was only offered in the evening. As I recall, it did not let out until 10 P.M. I didn't like the idea of her walking alone across the large parking lot that late at night. It didn't seem safe. I only agreed to her taking the night class if she would ask another student to walk her back to her car.

On the first night of class, she obediently asked one of her classmates to accompany her to the parking lot. As they were walking and getting acquainted, he asked what she was studying and if she knew yet what she wanted to do as a career. "Oh, yes I do know. I want to become a kindergarten teacher," she said.

He looked at her oddly and said, "What did you say your last name is?"

"Munson."

He looked surprised, "Is your mom a kindergarten teacher?"

"Yes, why?"

"I think she was my kindergarten teacher!" he laughed. "What a co-incidence. I went to Bear Street School."

When Dana got home that night, she told me what had happened and asked if I remembered a boy named Kevin from my time at Bear Street. He was a couple years older than her, so it would have been at least fifteen years ago.

Even at that point in my career I had already taught almost seven hundred children. After a while individuals blend together in your recollection. I could not remember them all. Yet, when I searched my memory, I thought I could put a face with the name Kevin. I recalled a little head covered with dark glossy curls. I was curious to see if my mental picture was accurate or not. So, I rummaged around in the closet to find a scrapbook containing pictures from my old school. Finally, I located a class picture with Kevin's name listed under it. Sure, enough his most prominent feature was a head full of beautiful brunette curls.

The next week when Dana went back to class, she informed Kevin that I did indeed remember him and that I had even found his picture. She said that seemed to please him. He continued to walk her to her car each week. After they got better acquainted, he asked her out.

On the night he came to our home to pick her up for the date, I stayed in the living room, but it was Dana who opened the front door. There stood a tall, slim, grown-up Kevin. Gone were the beautiful curls, replaced by nicely combed wavy hair. He had grown into a handsome young man. Dana welcomed him in. In his hand he was holding a bouquet of beautiful red roses. He smiled at Dana when he said, "Don't get excited. These are not for you; they are for my teacher!" He turned and handed the roses to me!

Needless to say, I melted with pleasure. He certainly knew how to be charming. It is a total surprise that a five- year-old would remember you for over fifteen years. The next time he came to take Dana out, the gift he brought was for her. He had composed a song for her, played it on the piano and had brought her a tape of it. He was obviously very talented as well as thoughtful.

Even though I was favorably impressed, Dana, at the time, never went out with any boy more than three times. It was not long before she stopped dating Kevin. Although I never saw him again, I was pleased to see that he had grown into such a nice young man, kind and creative, and that he still remembered his kindergarten teacher. Although my time at Bear Street School is so long in the past, I know that I will always happily remember Kevin and his flowers for teacher.

A Small World

One of the things I liked best about teaching kindergarten was that it allowed you to do so many creative activities. The program encompassed music, dance, drama, literature and of course lots of arts and crafts.

I enjoyed teaching all of these subjects, but I think perhaps my favorite was art. When children came to school on the first day, they colored a picture of themselves. Invariably there were some self-portraits with just a circle for a face, with two squiggly lines for legs dangling down, and two sticks for arms protruding where ears should be, reflecting tentative little space aliens entering the world of art for the first time. Many had also never been allowed scissors before. One boy picked up a pair for the first time and didn't know what to do with them. Mystified, he held them up to his eyes to peer through the finger holes like spectacles. There were always a few who, when trying to cut out a circle, were dismayed when the scissors kept on cutting straight ahead, instead of following the line. The first time they squished their hand in finger paint they often looked at me with an anxious expression that clearly asked, "Is it really O.K. to make a mess?" The first thing to learn was how to handle the materials. Rules like: you don't drive a brush forward but pull it gently toward you. You need only a few drops of glue, not a whole puddle, etc.

Over the course of the year the children experienced a wide range of mediums. They used tempera paint, starch with finger paint, and watercolors. They did crayon resist, sponge painting, gadget printing, marble painting, scrafitto and spatter painting through screens. They used colored chalk, glue and paste. There was also paper sculpture, collage, and weaving. Of course, they also made things: picture frames of macaroni and tongue depressors, trucks from egg cartons, Christmas trees of cones frosted with whipped soap flakes, drums from oatmeal cartons, masks, and mobiles. Some projects were unusual, starched string wound around a balloon, left to dry and harden before popping the balloon. Or they would let a snail crawl around construction paper, later tracing the snail trail with silver paint. The list of art possibilities was endless.

Sometimes we did large class projects that all the children worked on. I bought a wood framed bulletin board and the kids spent hours carefully gluing, making a mosaic of beans and seeds that became a permanent piece of art to hang in the school. For two consecutive years the class made a large papier mâché animal. My partner teacher's husband constructed the wood frames, and the children added the strips of paper, dipped in starch, and finally painted Dandy Lion and Ferdinand the Bull. Both creations were exhibited in Newport Beach art shows held at Fashion Island. The city asked to keep Dandy Lion for the next year's planned show and Ferdinand the Bull was requested by the city library to be displayed as part of their summer reading program for children, so both went on to lead happy lives.

The district employed an art curriculum consultant who would occasionally come to class and teach a demonstration art lesson. I enjoyed her visits and picked up some good ideas from her. She was always very complimentary about our room, especially our mural. Every year I filled the long bulletin board across the front of the room with a mural that reflected the theme of whatever our current unit of study was. One year the theme was transportation. The sponge painted blue sky that stretched over 20 feet long was filled with childishly painted airplanes soaring above a variety of trucks and cars. The art consultant asked if she could have it and it was hung on display at the Orange County Airport.

My favorite mural was one inspired by a recent trip to nearby Disneyland. In 1966 Disney had added a new attraction called "It's a Small World." It was a ride that featured animatronic dolls in colorful costumes that reflected their cultures. The attraction's adorable moving dolls were almost the size of real kindergarten children. I loved it. Just like that, I had the idea for our next thematic mural. Although celebrating multicultural diversity was not especially common back then, that is what "a small world" was about. The mural gave rise to many classroom activities. The children brought international dolls from home to share and display in our classroom. We painted flags of the world. In January they made Eskimo children in an arctic environment. On St. Patrick's Day, they painted children wearing green, and shamrocks were added to the mural.

We didn't seem to have a lot of diversity within the class, although little Nancy Takata was from the Japanese family that owned the local nursery. We made Japanese fans and cherry blossom scrolls and learned a Japanese dance about springtime. One of the class mothers with a Scottish background brought in homemade shortbread for all to sample. I dreamed up an art activity where the children used rulers and bits of peeled crayons to create plaid designs. Another mother sent in wooden shoes from her childhood in Holland. We added spring tulips to the mural. My partner teacher Darlene liked to travel. She demonstrated how to wrap a sari as she modeled a beautiful blue and silver silk one from India. She also brought madras fabrics and carved woodblocks that we used with tempera paint to do woodblock printing. My Norwegian contribution was Berlinerkranzer wreath cookies and the folktale of *The Three Billy Goats Gruff*. We made goat headbands and dramatized the story using a long table as a bridge. The little goats would walk across, trip-trap, until the troll in his ugly mask would pop out from under the table to growl, "I'm going to eat you up!" Of course, we didn't ignore our neighbor Mexico, as we learned the Mexican Hat Dance, painted serapes from grocery bags, broke a pinata and added more painted children to the mural.

Of course, we learned the small world song: "It's a world of laughter, a world of tears. It's a world of hopes and a world of fears. There's so much that we share, that its time we're aware, it's a small world after all."

I had been teaching at Bear Street School for four years when I became pregnant. My baby was due during summer vacation, at the end of August. I applied for the then available year of maternity leave. It was approved and I would soon be leaving. Although excited about the pregnancy, I knew I would miss the world of kindergarten. I would miss the creativity, the art and fun, the songs sung by everyone, the world of laughter, the world of tears, the world of learning despite their fears. I would no longer share in that colorful joyous world filled with little people. I would definitely miss my small, small world.

Ferdinand

Dandy Lion

It's A Small World

Job Sharing

One of the factors I considered when choosing a career path was how it would fit in with having and raising children and fulfilling the role of wife and homemaker. Teaching seemed to offer the most compatibility with that.

As a teacher you have a long summer vacation to remain at home with your own children to do typical things like taking them to swimming lessons or on vacations. It was a bonus that a teaching schedule coordinated with your children's school holidays, so it was possible to be at home to supervise them. Although at the time it was common to just stop working once you had children, I thought it would be nice to have options.

I never planned for the fact that my first pregnancy would occur before I would even start teaching. My first teaching job lasted one semester. I only remained at home until I was rehired the following September. Since my salary was necessary, I taught for the next three years. You became a tenured teacher upon teaching the first day of your fourth year. That had not happened for me, as we moved to Alhambra after my husband graduated medical school. I also taught there just three years before divorcing and moving to the beach. In 1971, I finally became a tenured teacher as I began my fourth year in the Newport-Mesa School District. Three years into my second marriage it was also the year I again became pregnant.

At the time, a year of maternity leave was available to tenured teachers. After taking a year off without salary I would be able to return to my job. Although my baby was due in the middle of August, it was a good thing that I had obtained the maternity leave, as I stayed contentedly pregnant until the third of September on Labor Day weekend. I was still in the hospital when school began.

The school year went by quickly and I had to let the district know if I would be returning or not. That was a difficult decision, as I loved teaching, but this was a chance to stay home with my new baby. I let the district know I would not be back. I chose to remain at home with our baby girl. I thought I had made the right decision. Life was perfect, until a day in November when my husband went to the doctor for a check-up. He was diagnosed with a particularly dangerous form of cancer. Duane was scheduled for immediate surgery to remove the tumor. We were in shock!

The doctors felt the surgery went well, but the news was by no means good. The prognosis for that type of cancer was an eighty percent fatality rate, generally within the first year. Duane was young, only twenty-nine, and otherwise in good health. He was able to return to his job after a couple weeks at home. But we didn't know how long he would be able to work, or if the cancer would return. I could not imagine any outcome other than a successful recovery, but to be cautious, we needed another income. I met with my former principal to discuss the problem. Fortunately, he offered a solution. The teacher who had filled my kindergarten position was pregnant and was due to begin a six-month maternity leave in January. I would be hired as a long-term substitute for her. I returned to my old classroom. Once again, the district was taking care of me.

Mrs. Sharman gave birth to a little boy and in June it was time for her to let the district know if she would return in September. She was facing the same tough decision I had made a year ago. She came to me with an idea. She had been reading an article in a women's lib magazine. It pointed out that women are at a disadvantage in the job field. They often have to choose to interrupt their careers due to pregnancy or stop working entirely to raise a young child. The article discussed job sharing as a possible solution to this problem. Ceil asked if I would be agreeable to trying such an arrangement. It sounded good to me.

We ended up writing a proposal to the school district for a split contract. Each of us would be awarded a fifty per cent contract but would still receive full benefits. To allay this extra expense, we would cover absences for each other to save the district the cost of substitutes. We listed the possible advantages to the plan and the district agreed to try it for a year as an experiment. That was how we initiated the first shared contract in the district.

The arrangement worked out well. I taught Mondays, Tuesdays, and every other Wednesday. Ceil taught Thursdays, Fridays and alternate Wednesdays. I did all report cards, cum folders and conferencing for the girls and Ceil took the boys. We subbed for each other when we or our children were ill. The negative, of course, is we were working at half salary, but that was more than compensated for by the extra days we got to spend with our babies in that precious year. For the next school year Ceil decided she would like a full income and preferred to return to an upper grade. Since Duane's health was still uncertain, I decided to return to a full-time position in kindergarten

Attached is a copy of an article from the Daily Pilot, Nov. 1974. The district continued to allow teachers to share contracts in the following years. In fact, when my daughter was in the third grade in Newport, she had two teachers who were sharing their job. I had to smile, since I guess we started something.

They Share Teaching

Bear Street School Instructors Trade Off Class

By HILARY KAYE
Of the Daily Pilot Staff

When school began in September, two kindergarten teachers at Costa Mesa's Bear Street School would meet and compare their classes.

"My class did well today in painting," Glenda Munson would say.

"And my class was well behaved," Lucille Sharman would remark.

It wasn't until a week had gone by that the teachers realized they should be referring to "our class," not "my class," because they were talking about the same children.

Mrs. Munson and Mrs. Sharman are part-time teachers who share the same kindergarten students at the Costa Mesa school.

They call their part-time arrangement "partnership teaching."

Mrs. Munson teaches Mondays, Tuesdays and alternate Wednesdays, while Mrs. Sharman takes over the rest of the week.

That way, both can divide their time between teaching and taking care of their own children at home.

Mrs. Munson, who leaves her 2-year-old child with a sitter when she teaches, says sharing the job gives her more time and energy.

Mrs. Sharman agrees, "I really look forward to my days of teaching. I'm turned on to the job and the kids."

The mother of a two-month-old baby and a 4-year-old, Mrs. Sharman says not only is she fresher on her teaching days, but that her teaching is richer, now that it's shared.

For the kindergartners, partnership teaching means little more than having certain subjects taught by certain teachers.

"Lucille is great with woodworking but I'm not. So I just tell the kids to leave their woodworking tools until it's Mrs. Sharman's day," says Mrs. Munson, laughing.

"And I'm not too good at art, while Glenda is a very good artist. So, that's her specialty," Mrs. Sharman says.

Mrs. Munson also teaches music and reading readiness. Mrs. Sharman emphasizes math and physical education.

Both agree that the sharing arrangement is good for both them and the kids, because they aren't forced into teaching areas they aren't personally interested in.

Students in their class see nothing unusual about having their week split up between the two teachers.

"That way, each one gets a turn," Kevin Khataturian, 5, explained nonchalantly.

Kevin said he wasn't surprised at having two teachers because he had quite a few in nursery school, too.

The team-teaching approach causes more paperwork, because each teacher leaves the other one the day's lesson plan, plus a complete rundown on what happened that day in class.

But other kinds of paper work, such as doing report cards and files, are cut in half.

School officials were skeptical of the arrangement at first, until the teachers wrote a proposal outlining their plan. Another influencing factor was the teachers' broad experience.

Mrs. Munson, a 12-year veteran, has taught at Bear Street four years, while Mrs. Sharman, who has taught eight years, has been at the school three and a half years.

ERIC GOELMAN, 5, SHARES LAUGH WITH TEACHERS
Glenda Munson (left), Lucille Sharman Share Class

Adventures in Substituting

I taught kindergarten full time for another couple of years. My husband's health improved after radiation treatment. He was apparently cured! I decided again to stay home with my young daughter so I could volunteer in her pre-school and kindergarten. Somehow years slipped by. Just when she was ready for a longer school day, and I was about to go back to work, I got pregnant once again with our son Michael.

Finally, when he was age nine, I was ready to return to teaching. I thought getting a job would be as easy as it had been in the past. I would just go down and apply for a contract. However, my former principal at Bear St. was no longer available as a reference; he had passed away. I went to the district office, filled out an application and met with the personnel director. Things had changed. He told me there were no openings at this time and that the district had in fact laid off some teachers. There was now a RIF (reduction in force) list, and any new hires would need to be filled first from that list. It was not encouraging.

The only option was to substitute, something I had never done. It did not sound appealing, but it would generate a little supplemental income. I decided to try it. The first hurdle was getting on the substitute list. Apparently, that was also full. I filled out an application anyway to get on the waiting list. Then I called a friend that had taught at Bear Street and gone on to become a consultant in the district. I asked her to put in a good word. That worked. I was added to the sub list, even though the caller did not like the fact that I would only accept kindergarten assignments.

The phone would ring between six and six-thirty in the morning and I would be told the class and the school to go to. I am not a morning person. It was stressful having to pop up immediately, shower, shampoo, dress, look up directions to a new school and arrive there no later than eight. But substituting was the path to a future contract.

I'll never forget my awful first day. The phone call at 6:00 A.M. sounded loud and shrill, interrupting and cutting short a blissful sleep. I did already know where the school was located. Newport Elementary was on the peninsula a short drive from my house, but even arriving early, the parking was scarce. It took me a precious fifteen minutes before I located a vacant place on the busy street. The secretary gave me directions to the kindergarten room and handed me the key.

I rushed down the hall and unlocked the door to the big kindergarten room. That is when my problems got worse. Lesson plans are supposed to be left on the teacher's desk. I searched the entire big room. There was no desk. I felt a whisper of panic. What was I supposed to do with thirty-five-year-olds all day? I only had about ten minutes left before they would arrive. Then I noticed the teacher work room, a glassed-in enclosure. I went in to look for supplies and, surprise, there in a corner was the desk! It held lesson plans and a couple stacks of worksheets. I had just time to skim quickly through them before the line of bus students filed noisily through the door. Did I mention that it was the first week of school? These children had not yet had time to learn a routine and it was uncontrolled chaos. I finally managed to herd them over to the rug and take attendance. None of them knew the way to the office so I had to keep the roll card to turn in later. There was no set of nametags, so I didn't know anyone's name, which made keeping control much more difficult. Perhaps I had forgotten how after being off for many years. Several children continued to be noisy and misbehave no matter what I said.

I thought recess on the kindergarten playground would provide a welcome relief, but it was worse. Their yard bordered the beach. There was no lock on the gate, just a close-up view of the big crashing waves. I have always been a worrier. What if a child managed to get out and ran into the surf? On the beach there were no lifeguards on duty. (I am a good swimmer but maybe not so able to rescue someone in giant waves.) I stood close to the gate ready to head any strays off at the pass. I also kept the door closed when we returned to the classroom. The knowledge that I was responsible for the safety of all these children was weighing heavily on me. At the end of the day, as I tried to get them lined up to go home with all their belongings, one little boy bolted out the door. I couldn't call out his name. I didn't know it. I couldn't chase him as I needed to stay with the rest of the class. I assumed he was headed for the waiting bus but with the waves in mind, I called the office to let them know about the escapee. I doubted I would get called back to this school again. (If I did, I doubted I would accept.) I was so glad when the terrible day was finally over. So far, I did not like substituting.

At first, I was not called often, perhaps once a week or less. Each time was an adventure. I never knew where I would be or what I would encounter. I discovered many teachers left no lesson plans, perhaps because they didn't know they would wake up too sick to come in. I learned to improvise. All I really needed was a time schedule to let me know about recess, arrival, and dismissal. One teacher forgot to mention that her students did not come to the room but waited by the bus on the other side of the campus. I finally found them.

Several classes were bilingual. I hadn't used my Spanish in many years, but I began to listen carefully for the last word in an otherwise too rapid question from a child. That was the clue to guessing their request, uttered in a combination of baby talk and Spanish. Something like blah, blah, blah *agua?* (Could they get a drink?) Blah, Blah *afuera?* (Could they go outside?) Blah, blah, blah *mi camisa?* (Would I button their paint shirt?) I started to recall my high school Spanish. One day I was sent to a very unusual assignment. I was told that the teacher of the class was being transferred to another school. She had already packed up her materials and left to set up her new classroom. Tomorrow this class would be split up and assigned to other rooms. I was shown to the classroom. It was almost completely bare, with only tables and chairs remaining. The bulletin boards were stripped. Toys and manipulatives were gone. There were a few picture books, a couple boxes of broken crayons and a small stack of coloring paper. "By the way," the principal informed me, "most of them do not understand English. This is a bilingual class and instruction has been in Spanish." Then she left. I don't believe anyone had informed the sub caller about that. I know she had no idea that I had any ability to speak Spanish. I improvised quickly and passed out a sheet of blank paper which we folded in half again and again. I demonstrated writing a numeral in each of the eight squares and let them color *tres cosas* in the box with *numero tres* and so on. Fortunately, that took a long time. We sang songs and I read simple Spanish books, but I have never had a day drag by so slowly, minute by boring minute.

Another day was also strange and unexpected. When I got to that school, I was told the class was scheduled to go on a field trip. We were to leave on a bus in fifteen minutes. I ran to the class and hunted up some bright red yarn. When the children arrived, I quickly tied a colorful bow around their wrists. Fortunately, a classroom aide showed up to help. She would be accompanying us on our boat cruise of Newport Harbor. We joined the other kindergarten class and piled onto a bus which took us to the Pavilion where we loaded sixty-five-year-olds onto the top deck of the waiting boat. There was bench seating around the edge of the deck and the main challenge was to keep everyone seated. They kept popping up from the bench like popcorn and leaning over the side of the boat. I kept tugging the backs of jackets and sweaters to keep them from going over. I had visions of having to leap from the top deck into the cold water of the bay. Unlike my first day of subbing, at least it was the bay and not the ocean. I was a bit more confident in my ability to act as a lifeguard. After the cruise, we walked around the fun zone. Half the class seemed unable to pass the arcade without wandering in. Thankfully, I was able to spot all the bright red bows and herd them together again. With a sigh of complete relief, I counted thirty little heads as they piled back into the bus, fortunately I was returning the same number I left with!

Some stressful moments actually turned out to be funny. One morning I was called in to a class where the teacher had left very complete plans. But even the best plans can miss mentioning an important detail. The table was already set up and prepared for the main activity of the day. There were sheets of manila paper with a large letter 0 drawn in black and bottles of glue were at each place. The children were to learn about the letter O and glue cheerios onto the numeral, a nice simple and time-consuming activity. The one catch was, try as I might, I couldn't find the cereal. I searched everywhere for fifteen minutes. When I was down to ten minutes before the children arrived, I decided I had to come up with an alternate activity. I quickly located some green construction paper and used the paper cutter to chop it lengthwise into 4" strips. I would have the children color insects and spiders along the paper and fringe the top edge with scissors to finish their strip of "grass" and reward them with insect stickers that I carried for just such an emergency. Breathless, I hurried and just finished resetting the table by eight-thirty when the class arrived. As they marched in the door, followed by the arriving teacher's aide, I noticed that under her arm she was carrying, you guessed it, a large box of Cheerios!

I learned as I went along. I began to carry a "goody" bag with me. In it I had plain white stickers that I could use as nametags that would not fall off. I had materials for an emergency art activity, a couple favorite storybooks, and lots of colorful stickers. Used as a behavior reward, these could always buy me a few minutes of attention. I also brought cute memo pads to label the completed work I left on the teacher's desk, and

personalized stationery, (for leaving a nice letter to the teacher). I also would dust the classroom and neaten the bookshelf before I left, kind of like a helpful cleaning lady. It was not long before teachers began requesting me in advance. The sub caller would let me know, so I was no longer awakened by those early morning calls. I was getting lots of work, often going back to the same schools on a regular basis. So, somehow, I made it through my first stressful year as a substitute teacher. However, I did not want to continue being a substitute, just filling in for a teacher. I wanted to be the real thing. My goal was to be **the teacher**!

College Park

I had completed a year of substituting. It had proved to not be nearly as satisfying as regular teaching. It did provide a part-time income, but the main thing I had hoped for was that it would lead to a full-time job. To my disappointment that had not happened by the end of summer. Ever hopeful, in September I again went on the sub list. Most teachers, especially those in kindergarten, try not to be absent at the beginning of the school year. So, it was October before I finally received a call to a kindergarten assignment.

It was at College Park, an elementary school in a quiet residential neighborhood in central Costa Mesa. It had a large kindergarten room, half of a separate building with an attached playground. I was called on a Wednesday and had an easy day, although there were no lesson plans left, just a time schedule. It was an afternoon kindergarten in a room shared with a morning teacher who was helpful. As I was finishing the day, the office called with a message from the sub caller to return the next day. I readily agreed, as it meant I could avoid the uncertainty of an early morning sub call. The same thing happened the following day, but assignments are automatically canceled on Friday afternoons.

On Monday morning I received an early morning call to return to the same class. At the end of each day, the office would again let me know to return the next day. This went on for the remainder of the week. It got easier as I got to know the children and became familiar with their routine. I received a request to continue in the class for another week. The teacher was going into the hospital for major surgery. The weekly assignments continued except for automatic cancellations over Thanksgiving and Christmas vacations.

I began taking over all the duties of a regular teacher including long term planning, conferences, report cards, holiday programs, field trips and open house. The teacher continued to be ill and was undergoing chemotherapy for cancer. I felt sympathy for her although I had never met her. Sometime in the Spring, I was told that she would not be returning, and my assignment would continue for the rest of the year. Once you sub for 100 days in a school year you are automatically reclassified as a long-term sub. I think I reached that point sometime in April. It meant a slightly higher salary rate per day for the remainder of the year and contributions to retirement.

I settled into the routine of a full-time teacher. One thing about teaching the afternoon class is that you have a different lunch time than the rest of the staff. Each day I ate lunch with only the other afternoon teacher, a young single girl named Suzy. We shared teaching ideas. I also heard the ongoing refrain of "there are no good single men left out there." Until one day she bubbled, "I met Mr. Right." Next, I heard about the proposal and the wedding plans. We had become friends sharing that kindergarten lunch hour. I gave a bridal shower at my home and filled in for her mom on the search for the wedding gown for the June wedding.

I also liked the morning teacher, Jamie, with whom I shared the room. We planned an extensive unit for open house and filled the room with the children's colorful artwork. I tried to make the year special for the children even though they had a sub. We went on field trips to the zoo in Santa Ana and to the farm at the Orange County Fairgrounds.

My husband came to school one day as a guest speaker. His job was Director of Human Resources for the City of Newport Beach. He told the children that lots of daddies go to work every day at all kinds of different jobs. He explained by bringing a lot of hats into the room and said his job was to fill those hats with people: gardeners, trash collectors, policemen, firemen, office workers and lifeguards. The children loved trying on the different hats and imagining what kind of work they might like to do when they grew up.

My daughter also came into our class. College Park was located very near to Orange Coast College, a community college where Dana was in her second year of preparing to be a teacher. She would come in to help with class activities to gain experience. Usually, she helped with art, but one other activity stands out in my memory. For learning about letter B, we held a pajama party where all the children could bring a bear to cuddle. Dana brought her giant bear and also wore pajamas. She helped the kids glue beans on a letter B and bake brownies. Somehow that got written up in an article in the district newsletter.

I got to know the principal, Dick Clark, and would tell him about our special activities. I hoped he would remember me when an opening on staff occurred. However, when the school year ended the kindergarten enrollment was still at a number too low to justify three kindergartens, and Dick Clark retired.

Over the summer the teacher I had subbed for sadly passed away. When a third class did finally fill, the district hired a young teacher straight out of school with no experience, but she was bilingual in Spanish. Being a long-term sub had been an improvement over ordinary subbing. Steady work and being able to plan had been much better than daily uncertainty. It meant an improvement in salary and the satisfaction of getting to know the children. I had also made new friends. However, after two years of subbing, I was still no closer to my goal of a contract.

Welcome to Wilson

No further openings occurred over the summer. Once again, I was preparing to go on the sub list. It was discouraging. In the past it had always been so easy to get a job, twice in South San Francisco, then in Alhambra, and twice in Newport Mesa. Now it felt almost impossible. I considered whether I should just give up on my quest for a teaching position and return to being a fulltime homemaker. However, my daughter had just graduated from Orange Coast College and transferred to U.C. Irvine. Her college costs were going to go up. So far, I was attempting to pay those entirely out of my earnings. My income would be even more necessary. I needed a job.

Just prior to the start of the school year my telephone rang with a significant call. It was from Dick Clark, the former principal of College Park who had retired in June. He was now the acting principal at Wilson School, filling in for their principal who was out following surgery. He was requesting me for a kindergarten position that had just opened at Wilson due to increased enrollment. The only catch was I would once again be employed as a long-term sub. Although, I would not actually be subbing for anyone. If he were to hire someone on a contract, he would be required to fill the opening from the RIF list, which currently had no one on it with any kindergarten experience. I thanked him and readily accepted. It was not ideal because I would be paid as a sub, but a steady income was welcome. I would finally have my very own class. I hoped it would lead to a contract for the next year.

Wilson school was located in Costa Mesa not far from College Park. I was assigned an afternoon kindergarten class located in a building housing two large rooms. Both rooms had tiled areas containing sinks and bathroom stalls and were connected by a teacher workroom and bathroom. The classrooms opened onto a separate kindergarten playground with lawns, and a huge shade tree. I was to share a classroom with the morning teacher named Edie. She taught a class of preschool children as part of the Migrant Education program. I wondered how that would turn out, with different age groups sharing the same space and materials, but surprisingly it went well. I enjoyed working with Edie. She was easy to get along with and often gave me good ideas. We both liked art and collaborated on an elaborate ocean unit for open house, filling the room with colorful sea creatures and a mural topped by two boatloads of smiling faces.

The room next door was shared by two more kindergartens. The teachers were Eddy in the morning and Katie in the afternoon. You might think that having Edie and Eddy as the two morning teachers would be confusing, but they were spelled differently. Edie and I enjoyed sharing a room. On the other hand, Eddy was very anxious to have "her" room all to herself. I presented an obstacle to that plan for the following year. She was hoping I would not be hired so Katie could move to my room. She lobbied the principal toward that end.

As the year went on, I realized that the district was under increasing pressure to hire bilingual teachers or teachers who held a Language Development Specialist credential. To make myself more employable, I decided to get the LDS certification. It required at least six units of any foreign language at the college level as well as several other courses in language acquisition. I already had the language units as I had taken a year of French at Pasadena City College long ago. I began taking the other required classes. I finished the last of the courses and passed the written exam toward the end of the summer. I was then certified as a language development specialist. By the end of the school year the enrollment had not yet come in for a third kindergarten. Katie was moved over to share my room with Edie. Eddy at last had her room to herself. My space had been filled.

I despaired of ever getting a contract. It was apparent that, in an effort to economize, the district was hiring young first year teachers straight out of school. It made sense. They were cheaper, as the more years of experience you have the higher you are on the salary scale. I realized that my experience was not only not valued, but was actually a handicap. It was an impediment because it made me a more expensive employee. I had now spent three years as a substitute. How was I ever going to get a contract?

It was my husband who came up with an answer. As the personnel director for the city of Newport Beach, he was quite familiar with the subject. "You are over fifty" he said, quite bravely mentioning that fact. "You could go to the Fair Labor Standards Board and claim age discrimination."

"But I don't think the problem is my age," I said.

"That doesn't matter," he stated. "If you make that claim, the district will have to prove that they do hire older teachers, which they probably can't. The statistics will support your case. Besides it is a lot of work for them to provide all those records. Just mention the words age discrimination. Believe me, they will hear you."

So, with some coaching beforehand, I called the school district personnel director and after being told that there were still no openings, I worked in the key phrases. "You know," I said, ever so politely, "if I didn't know better, I would think you are discriminating against me because of my age."

"Of course not," he denied. "There just haven't been any openings."

"Well," I said, "you filled the opening at College Park with a younger candidate when I was more qualified in every way. I have a better educational background, with a degree from UCLA, as well as a lifetime teaching credential. I also have exceptional references and experience at that grade level."

"Well, she was a native Spanish speaker," he countered.

"I also speak Spanish," I said. "No one tested me on that," I volunteered, as Duane had said they must do. "And, I am now certified as a Language Development Specialist," I offered. Mentioning that couldn't hurt. He hemmed and hawed a little, but I knew my message was getting through.

I don't know which remark made the difference, but during the following week I received calls from three different principals. One offered me a contract teaching an upper grade which I turned down. The other two calls were for interviews for kindergarten openings. The Wilson one came first. Enrollment had finally come in for a third kindergarten. The principal was pleased that I had gotten the LDS certificate and offered me a kindergarten contract. Finally! It was a goal achieved. I was happy to accept, even when she looked at me seriously and asked, "Glenda, are you sure you want to do this?" I nodded yes. "Why?"

She gave a hearty laugh, "Well, you will be sharing a room with Eddy!"

My kindergarten class at Wilson

Danny

Finally, I was offered a contract after three years of substitute teaching. I was hired as an afternoon kindergarten teacher at Wilson School. I was so happy to finally be returning to fulltime teaching. However, that year proved to be a sometimes difficult one. Wilson was on an alternate schedule starting in August, so classes had already been in session for a month. Enrollment had continued to straggle in. The two existing kindergartens were up to 45 students each, enough to enable forming a third class. The other kindergarten teachers were each directed to select 15 students to place in the new class. Selection was supposed to be random but as every teacher knows, if you have a difficult student or two in your class, it is a great temptation to pass the problem on to someone else.

I like to give them the benefit of the doubt, but for whatever reason, that class proved to be difficult. Perhaps it was just because I had not begun the year with them. The first weeks of school are essential in establishing your classroom rules and routine. Whatever the cause, I felt like I was often struggling with control.

Sometimes it just takes one child to disrupt other students. One particular child from that class sticks out in my memory. Danny was an active boy with sandy blonde hair, rosy cheeks, and dimples. He liked things to go his way and often had trouble playing well with others. He also had a temper. One day during work time there was a loud commotion on the rug where several boys were busy building with blocks and Legos. Danny and a couple other boys were arguing. I stepped in to stop the fight from coming to blows and told the group to clean up and choose another activity. The others complied but Danny was enraged and red in the face. He continued to protest and shout. He was crying so hard that it was difficult to understand what he was yelling about or what he wanted. In minutes his tantrum escalated. He threw himself on the floor and began wailing even louder while kicking his feet and pounding the rug with his fists.

When he began banging his forehead against the floor, I decided to send him to the principal to let him cry it out. The custodian came and carried Danny out. At recess I went over to the office where the secretary filled me in on their afternoon. They had tried having him sit in a chair in the office waiting area, but the bloodcurdling screams were too distracting. Next, he was moved to the adjacent nurse's office and the glass door between was shut. The screaming could still be heard, so he was put in the tiny sick room where he could rest on a cot. The tantrum continued, but this time there were two closed glass doors between him and the office staff. The secretary said it was still impossible for the staff to hear anyone over the phone because of the volume. They wondered what terrible thing had happened to set him off.

"I don't have any idea!" I said. By now he was somewhat exhausted. The screaming had changed to quieter sobs. I went into the sick room and asked him what had happened. "Danny what made you so upset with the other boys?"

He looked at me with his mottled red face and said indignantly, "They took the last green Lego!" I couldn't help but wonder that such a tiny thing had provoked such an extreme response. It was unusual. Most children have given up violent tantrums before kindergarten. Although I had previously encountered a few, they were usually shorter in duration.

During the ensuing parent conference, we discussed temper tantrums. I suggested to the parents that children often do it as a means of getting their own way and if that tactic no longer works, they often outgrow them. Perhaps they might try rewarding good behavior instead of giving in to the tantrums. I remember saying that, in my opinion, it was important to effect change in behavior now, while he was still young, and they were still the adults in charge. "In a few years gaining control will be much more difficult!" I warned. I hoped that conference would help.

Danny and his family moved away at the end of that school year. Several years later, I was walking across the playground when a boy came walking toward me. I was just back from a two year leave of absence and did not recognize him. Our school only went up to the fifth grade, but this stranger was taller than I was. He came right up to me, threw his arms around me, and hugged me. "Teacher," he said' "you're back!"

When I saw his happy smile, I remembered him. It was Adrian, one of the boys from Danny's class. He was a large boy that had been as big as a third grader in kindergarten, but he was a gentle giant with the sweetest disposition. He had grown and now this fifth grader almost looked like he could make a high school football team in the near future. "Do you remember me from kindergarten?" he asked. When I assured him I did, he said, "Do you know who else is back this year?"

His eyes were wide with amazement. "You remember Danny" he went on, "how mean he was? Well, he's back. He's bigger now, but he's still mean!" Apparently, Danny was continuing to have trouble getting along with the other kids. I had hoped that would improve. Sometimes change is hard to bring about.

It is easy at first to think of kindergarteners as just babies, but they are actually little people that have had five years or so to develop personality traits before they ever come to school. That makes each one of them unique and interesting.

Years later I attended a reunion of retired teachers from my former school, Bear Street. The teachers were older than I. They began reminiscing about a kid way before my time there. "Do you remember Billy ____?" they asked. Many of them did. He had misbehaved at every grade level, fought a lot, and was often expelled.

"Well," one of them said, "I just read about him in the paper. He became a serial killer, murdered eight people and is now in prison on death row!" There was silence in the room for a minute and I know each of those teachers was sadly remembering a difficult little boy that they wished they could have helped.

Conference Time

Parent teacher conferences took place twice during the school year, November and again in spring. A week was designated conference week with no student attendance on Wednesday. Teachers held as many conferences as possible on Wednesday and fit in the rest after school on the other days of the week. It meant staying late which took away from time usually spent in lesson preparation. For the first few years I taught it was almost impossible to conference with every parent as I had two classes of students. Maximum enrollment was thirty-five in a class. One year I had seventy students. With twenty minutes allowed for each conference I could do three an hour. Even with an eight-hour day with no lunch, I could only get through a third of my students. With two hours a day after school the other four days I could do another third and the rest spilled over to the following weeks. If the parent didn't show I did not make any effort to reschedule. It just took too much time away from setting up for each day's activities, already time consuming at kindergarten level.

I used the November conferences to let the parent know how their child was adjusting to school and to explain the report card and learning goals for the year. In the spring I showed them the scope of their child's progress. Conferences were a time to build rapport with the parents and make sure they were pleased with their child's experience. I tried to answer questions they might have and smooth over any problems. One conference stands out in my memory. It was a mom at Ramona school who had an older child at the school but had also just given birth two months earlier. She was nervous and visibly upset. She talked rapidly and seemed constantly on the verge of anger. I told her that her child had adjusted nicely and was doing well in class, attempting to reassure her. Finally, she calmed down. After an hour, I gently guided her towards the door and her anger flared up every now and then but did not seem directed at me. She never did define what the problem was but kept rambling. A week later I heard she had burst into the auditorium during a promotion ceremony, gone to the stage, and started yelling while wheeling around in circles. The police were called. She was admitted to a mental hospital and diagnosed with postpartum schizophrenia. The conference with her was the most puzzling I have ever held.

When I began teaching at College Park in Costa Mesa, it was the first time I encountered parents who did not speak English. This added a new challenge to conferences. Parents were not as likely to show up for their appointment, often because they did not speak English. One day I was waiting after school for an appointment to come, this one was late. I happened to look out the window and noticed the father standing way outside the kindergarten yard, over on the upper grade playground. I wondered if he was confused about where to come. I walked out to where he was. He did not speak any English, so I did my best in Spanish inviting him to come in. He appeared embarrassed and made no move in the direction of the room. I thought perhaps there was a problem with my Spanish and, wording it another way, I told him that it was time for his conference. He hung his head down and confessed in Spanish that he couldn't come because he didn't have enough money. What? I was sure I was translating correctly, but his answer didn't make any sense. He didn't need *dinero*. Taking a chance, I said, "*La conferencia es gratis.*" (The conference is free.) It worked. He smiled and relaxed and began walking with me toward the room. Somehow, we made it through the conference with my Spanish, but I never did solve the mystery of the problem.

Another odd misunderstanding occurred when I was at Wilson School. I was in the middle of a conference with Gustavo's mother. She was a nice lady who spoke English well. It was after we had been speaking for a while that she commented about Adolfo. Wait. I thought this was Gustavo's mom. Confused, I checked my appointment sheet, yes, Gustavo. But she was chatting on about Adolfo. Had we been talking all this time about the wrong kid? Should I fess up and admit it? Acutely embarrassed, I spoke up, "I'm so sorry, I thought you were Gustavo's mom."

"Oh, I am," she said. "But I am Adolfo's grandmother." Surprised, I recalled the way the two boys always sat next to each other on the rug. Who knew that Adolfo was sitting next to his five-year-old uncle Gustavo.

Conferences proved to be educational, for me that is. I learned to see things from a new perspective. I often caught a glimpse of the struggles that parents were facing. Our viewpoints differed. I was concerned about the ABC's; the parents were concerned about surviving. I encouraged one mom to read to her daughter at bedtime to help her learn, meanwhile wondering why she didn't. The mother admitted that she was not able to. Every night after dinner she dressed her daughter in her pajamas and put her in the backseat of their car to fall asleep while she had to drive the father to his job as a night watchman.

Another mother of one of my best students confided that they were about to move to Santa Ana. "The rent in Santa Ana is cheaper than Costa Mesa," she said. In Costa Mesa there were three families sharing their apartment with only one bathroom. One of the other families had teenage girls who would not come out of the bathroom when her son needed to use it. He had wet his pants waiting for a turn. She said a couple of the men spent the evening drinking beer and being boisterous until after midnight, keeping her son awake. (I hated to lose him as a student.)

At the end of each conference, I needed to have the parent place their signature on the bottom of the report card. One day when I came to that point with Francisco's father, he hesitated, became embarrassed and admitted to me that he couldn't write his name. He explained that where he grew up in Mexico he had not ever gone to school. The translator explained to him that he could make an X. Blushing a bit, he laboriously made a shaky X. While he did, everything inside me was ready to blurt out that he needed to come in after school and I would teach him to write his name, but I knew that would just make him more embarrassed, so I remained quiet.

Conferences are meant to bridge the gap between home and school. The thing is, sometimes it is not just a gap, but a huge gulf, one that stretches across international borders, cultures, and languages. The span yawns over poverty and ignorance below, but perhaps education is building a bridge.

When he was ready to leave, Francisco's dad kept smiling and thanking me repeatedly, "Gracias, gracias!" I wondered why, but then I noticed he still held the work samples I had given him, one of them a page where Francisco had laboriously written out his name in large childlike printing. He had already learned to sign his signature!

Miranda

You never know what a five-year-old is going to think of next. The possibilities are too varied to guess. Kids never cease to surprise me, not always in a good way. The time when students are the calmest and most attentive is when they are all seated together on the rug. The kindergarten carpet is an area rug with rows of bright primary colors divided into squares. Each child sits in their own square with legs and hands folded. Since they are sorted and somewhat still, this is the ideal time to read a story or present a lesson. It needs to be short as their attention span, even under ideal conditions, is about twenty minutes. Half an hour is pushing it. After that the wiggles and giggles set in. In the meantime, the unexpected sometimes occurs.

Miranda was one of the brightest students in my class, perhaps the politest and best behaved. She was not normally one to interrupt or cause problems, but one day in the middle of story time she raised her hand, waving it wildly and calling out, "Teacher, teacher!"

"What is it, Miranda?" I asked, wondering what couldn't wait until the end of the story.

"A bean is stuck in my ear!" she announced.

If it were any other child I would have guessed they were making it up. But Miranda was very mature and reliable, so I stopped reading to question her.

"How did it get there?" Gradually she explained. We had been playing a game earlier with beanbags. Hers had a tiny hole in it through which she managed to squeeze out a bean. What do you do with a bean when you go to the rug for story time? Why you find a place to put it, of course. Perhaps in a tiny hole, like the one in her ear for instance. It seemed like an opening of just the right size for a tiny bean. The only problem was she couldn't get it back out. The more she tried the further in it went.

After patiently eliciting the whole story from Miranda I took a look in her ear. I could indeed see a bean wedged inside her ear, way inside her ear. I decided this situation was beyond my capability and sent her over to the school nurse for more expert help.

I returned to reading the story. Of course, by this time more that twenty minutes had gone by, and boredom was beginning to set in for some. I looked up from reading aloud to notice that two of the youngest boys were giggling and whispering with their heads bent together. I observed that they had the flys of their jeans undone and were both busy comparing their penises.

Although I was shocked, the rest of the class seemed oblivious to what was going on. My first thought was, "Don't react!" so in a matter of fact voice I calmly said, "Juan, Jose, we do not do that in kindergarten" and then continued reading. They seemed surprised and embarrassed at being discovered, and they obediently zipped up. I finished the story and none of the rest of the class seemed to have noticed the cause of the interruption. However, I had to try very hard not to laugh. As I said, you never know what a five-year-old will do next.

At recess I checked on Miranda with the office. The nurse had also decided against trying to retrieve the bean, fearing to push it in further. She called Miranda's mother who took her to a doctor. He was able to delicately retrieve the bean with some surgical tweezers and Miranda returned to class none the worse for her experience. Years later, Miranda sticks in my memory like the bean that was stuck in her ear.

Before the class was dismissed that afternoon, I had a little talk with them explaining that tiny things like beans, pebbles, beads, and Legos should never be put into their ears or their nose. It was always a bad idea because they might get stuck. Then, like Miranda, they might even have to get help from a doctor.

With all the unexpected interruptions I'm not sure the children absorbed the story I read or would remember anything positive from the lesson that day, but perhaps some of them learned about what was not appropriate to do, especially Miranda, and hopefully Juan and Jose!

Another Kevin

The first day of kindergarten is often traumatic for children, especially if they have not attended preschool. Over the years I saw a wide range of reactions from tears and quiet sobbing to full-fledged screaming tantrums. I learned to take them in stride as they rarely lasted more than a few minutes before the terror subsided.

However, one first day memory stands out in my mind. I was teaching in a bilingual school that year. All of my students spoke Spanish as their first language and some had never encountered English before. I knew that would add another element to their fear of school if they could not understand anything the teacher was saying. Consequently, I tried to use both languages to welcome them at first, but I am not fluently bilingual. I didn't know if that was adding to little Kevin's fear or not, but in the first few minutes before class he began throwing a noisy tantrum, shouting in Spanish that he was not going to stay. He was going home!

The children had lined up on the playground outside the classroom door. When it was time for the class to go inside, Kevin turned to run. I held tight to his hand as we waved goodbye to the parents. I led him inside where he began kicking and screaming and then went limp. I had to pick him up off the floor and carry him to the rug where the class was seated.

I have found that it is usually best to ignore a tantrum. Most children that throw them have found in the past that it is an effective tool in getting their way. In fact, the louder and wilder it is the better it succeeds, so they learn to escalate. However, when they find those tactics don't work at school, they usually quiet down, and the tantrum subsides. Not so with Kevin. He continued to cry and scream at the top of his lungs. He howled all during our good afternoon song, and the flag salute, and counting numbers on the calendar, and sharing, and games. The other children kept looking at him with wide-eyed astonishment. Fortunately, the tears were not contagious, as they sometimes are on the first day of school.

So far, this behavior did not make Kevin unique in my experience, but by the time we got to activity time where children could choose to paint or color, play with puzzles or Legos, or go in the playhouse, most kids would give it up and start to participate. Not Kevin, he continued to bawl loudly. While the other children were busy playing I went over and tried to talk to him and comfort him. It didn't work. He bolted for the door saying in Spanish that he was going to go home and never come back!

When he attempted to turn the knob and open the door of course I had to step in and stop him. Then I made the mistake of saying, "No!" I'm pretty sure he was not used to hearing that word at all. He went ballistic. He began to rush at the cabinets and kick them repeatedly as hard as he could. He tore off his tennis shoes and proceeded to throw them at the classroom windows, although not hard enough to break them. Then he screamed a long stream of Spanish at me. But, with all the sobbing he was doing I couldn't understand him. I asked the morning teacher, who was completely bilingual, to translate for me.

When she did I was surprised. "He says he is going to put out a hit on us. His big brothers are in a gang, and they will come and kill us both!"

I smiled and said, "Tell him that we are not afraid of his big brothers!"

That was true when I said it, as I pictured some third or fourth graders just laughing at his request. After school I happened to see the two burly high school brothers that came to pick him up. Their belted pants hung low on their hips. They sported tattoos to go with their piercings. Perhaps I spoke too soon.

For the next two days, Kevin continued to cry through our opening time, loud enough that the children next to him had to cover their ears. He was stubborn for sure. I continued to ignore the noise although it was difficult. On the fourth day of school I was attempting to take role despite the howling when one of the other boys raised his hand and said in a shy voice. "Maestra, he is crying." Like he thought I didn't notice.

I decided I had better try to explain. "Well I know he is, but let me tell you why. Some children don't know what kindergarten is like before they come here. They think it is a scary place until they find out how many things there are to do and how much fun it is. They sometimes cry at first because they are afraid." I glanced at Kevin wondering if he understood what I had just said. Then, the most amazing thing happened. He stopped crying in mid howl. In fact, his mouth hung open with no sound. I never heard another sob out of him. Inadvertently, I had said the magic word. He had grown up macho brothers that he idolized. Wanting to be just like them, he was determined that no one was ever going to think he was **afraid!** It turned out that although Spanish was his first language, he was also just as fluent in English and understood every word I had said, especially that one.

As the weeks progressed, Kevin bravely blossomed into one of my brightest and most capable students. He always wanted to sit close to me at story time and would often tell me, "I love you teacher!" I guess he reconsidered ordering the hit.

A Room Divided

My new assignment was far from ideal. It was as an afternoon kindergarten teacher, sharing a classroom with Eddy, the morning teacher. The room was next door to the classroom I had occupied the year before, with Edie, in the other half of the kindergarten building.

Both classrooms shared the connecting teacher workroom. It held the supply of tempera paints, chart paper, easel paper and construction paper, in addition to the paper cutter, a clothes closet, coffee maker, sink and a teacher restroom. The workroom and restroom were a great advantage of being in a separate kindergarten building.

Eddy had campaigned the previous year to <u>not</u> have me hired. That way the afternoon teacher currently in her room could move next door and Eddy would not have to share her classroom. She got her way over the summer, but it backfired. The enrollment climbed, and I was hired after all. Now, she was forced to share her room with me, instead of her friend who had already made the move.

Actually, I understood why she did not want to share her space. She had been there for years, and the room was stuffed! She liked to acquire things and keep them. It was a large room but nevertheless, it was full. In addition to the usual classroom tables, chairs and bookshelves, there were large bins containing: blocks, clay, toy vehicles, musical instruments, rubber dinosaurs and stuffed animals. There were extra furniture units for puzzles, charts, games, books, two large banks of cubbies, plus her desk, and an upright piano. One corner of the room was occupied by a large refrigerator. The tiled art area was filled by more furniture and a row of tall metal filing cabinets. Every built- in cupboard along the walls was jammed with her materials. I guess it was all useful stuff, but the room reminded me of a television episode of Hoarders. There was not much space for anything else.

Eddy announced that she had cleared a cupboard in the teacher's workroom, and I could have that. I thanked her but said I would need some space in the room as well. She didn't seem happy about that, but finally cleared out a piece of furniture that had shallow drawers with a vinyl top. It sat in the tiled area of the room between the kiddy sinks and potty stalls. "Since there's not room for another teacher desk, you can use this," she said.

The drawers were useful for my charts, calendars, and bulletin board supplies but the vinyl topped piece did not work as a desk. There was no room for a chair because it was too close to the bathroom stalls, so I could not sit to do my lesson planning, plus, the area smelled! I tried staging my lesson materials there, but they often got water splashed on them from the nearby sinks.

Finally, I quietly went to the principal and requested a teacher desk. When the custodian came wheeling it in, I deferred to Eddy as to where it should go. She wasn't pleased but finally gestured to a spot. I found myself in a crowded corner of the room sandwiched between the noisy playhouse and a row of computers and hidden behind tall metal carts that housed the school's projectors, T.V. and other bulky audio-visual equipment. I tried to keep most of my materials at home. I carried a basket back and forth each day with whatever I needed, in order to take up as little space as possible. I was trying to adjust to my new partner.

Most of the time we got along all right, but Eddy was determined to have "her" room to herself for more of the day. She was not only grade level chairman but the bilingual coordinator for the school. Wilson was scrambling to comply with new rules for instruction based on numbers of second language speakers. It was in the process of transitioning to a bilingual school. The principal did not speak Spanish and relied on Eddy to come up with a plan for compliance. Her plan for kindergarten called for an hour of instruction in Spanish. Since this impacted the largest number of students it would take place in the large kindergarten room and be taught by Eddy. During this same time, I would instruct the remainder of the students who spoke: English only, Vietnamese, Japanese, Chinese, and Tagalog. The only available space was an unused portable classroom way out on the back field. So, every day, we switched kids, and I was required to take my group of students on a long march across the big playground and up the noisy metal ramp to the empty portable. It was dark, dreary, and cold. Last used by an upper grade, the chairs and tables were too tall for the kindergartners. Since the room was empty of supplies, I was limited in the activities I could do there. I mostly toted paper, pencils, erasers, a few crayons, writing journals and a story book. The daily trek was a waste of instructional time and often cold, although at least it does not rain often in Southern California. I'm not sure its improved language acquisition any, but as far as Eddy was concerned it got me out of her room.

I began to think about a possible option. Right behind the kindergarten building there was another building, a row of classrooms mostly filled by first grades. However, the first room was used as the science room. All the school science kits, kept in big boxes, were stored there and teachers could schedule time to take their classes in and teach a science lesson. The room was infrequently used, as many teachers found it easier to check out a kit and take it to their own classroom. The space could be better utilized. I envisioned that it might work as a kindergarten. It was only steps from the back gate to the kindergarten yard.

It was worth a try. I wanted to move out of Eddy's overcrowded room. Eddy obviously wanted me out of "her" room. Didn't that put us on the same side? Our goals were one and the same and Eddy had a lot more pull with the principal who tended to be in favor of the "science room." I mentioned the idea to Eddy, who immediately saw the possibilities and agreed to work on it. We knew there would be obstacles to overcome, but I was sure Eddy could do it. We could work together toward a common goal.

I gazed around the big kindergarten room once more, with fresh eyes. There was certainly no place for my things. It was obvious **there was no room to spare; but there was a spare room!**

Room 11

After much persuasion, especially from Eddy, the principal finally gave in to the idea of doing away with the "science room" and letting room 11 be used as a kindergarten. However, she had one stipulation. She was not going to spend one penny of her budget on furnishing the room. I would have to figure that out for myself.

I was happy to escape the tension caused by sharing an overcrowded room with Eddy. However, I was not without a lot of doubt about the move. My biggest concern was the small size of the room. This would be my thirteenth year of teaching kindergarten, and I had always occupied a large room designed specifically as a kindergarten. Not only was room 11 just a regular sized classroom, but it was dark, dreary, and empty. It would present a challenge. Could I do it?

The first step was to get rid of all the science kits, stacks of large boxes that filled one wall of the room. The principal, Sandy, gave her permission to store them in the teachers' work room where they could be checked out for science lessons. Eddy arranged for a few strong sixth grade boys to help the custodian load them onto a cart and transport them. That was helpful of Eddy, but then, she really wanted her room to herself. They also removed all the classroom chairs as they were oversized for kindergarteners. Two worktables were adjustable, and the custodian lowered them to the appropriate height. There was one storage cabinet with drawers in the room, other furniture was non-existent!

The principal referred me to a room in the district that was used to store unused furniture. I visited and was amazed at the conglomeration of odd, broken, and shabby pieces that were available and mostly unusable. I did find two large stand-alone bookshelves that I requested. The custodian became interested in my project. He moved my nice, wooden teacher's desk from Eddy's room to my new room. I could have hugged him when he found me the only piano not otherwise in use in the school. It was even a blonde wood to match my desk.

I had storage for books now, but not enough shelves for classroom games and supplies that the children would need access to. I began to haunt the Salvation Army and Goodwill secondhand stores. Fortunately, I found a ready supply of used IKEA furniture which had been donated. I bought several low pieces with open shelves that had been television stands. They were scratched and wobbly, but they only cost two or three dollars each. My husband reinforced them with metal brackets and gave them a coat of white enamel paint. They worked perfectly below the bulletin boards and windows.

The room appeared very dark despite one wall of tall windows. One of the reasons was that the front wall of the room was taken up by a dark green chalkboard. I didn't have a use for that, but I did need more bulletin board space. With the principal's permission, my husband, Duane, installed sheets of cork over the chalkboard and finished it off with a frame of wood molding which he painted off-white. Contributing to a dark look were the existing built-in cabinets. The school was old, so they were a nice solid wood, instead of the ugly metal ones currently being installed, but they were worn and painted a dark tan color. The wall of built-in paint easle was framed in that same wood. Sandy also allowed us to change that. Duane and I came in over the summer and painted all the woodwork a creamy off white. The room looked so much brighter!

I invited the principal over to see the transformation. I think my excitement was contagious. I guess she was impressed, as she broke her own rule and spent money from her budget. I was surprised when two dozen new small chairs, a beautiful dark blue, were delivered to my room. Along with them came a kindergarten rug divided into colorful rows of squares, a very helpful tool for seating.

Another thing, essential in kindergarten, is for each child to have a cubby. A wooden piece of furniture divided into cubbies is prohibitively expensive to purchase, but more importantly, I did not have the space for one. Just inside the door, there was a low closet area with hooks for children to hang their backpacks and jackets. I got the district carpenter to come, remove the hooks and install a row of them for backpacks on the wall outside my classroom in the sheltered corridor. That left the closet area vacant. The other kindergarten teacher, Katie, came to the rescue. Her friend, Richard, was handy with woodwork and he custom made a bank of twenty cubby shelves that exactly fit into the opening. I painted it to match the cabinets to look built-in.

The only thing left to do was accessorize with finishing touches. I would miss the convenience of Eddy's classroom refrigerator, so I purchased a tiny frig designed for a dorm room that neatly tucked in the space between my piano and desk. I also found an antique wooden rocking chair at the Good Will store. It was painted in a soft cream color and was a perfect teacher chair. Next, I raided my garage, bringing things that my daughter had long since outgrown, to furnish the playhouse area, including a doll bed, a small table and chairs, a little stove my husband had built, and dolls and dishes. I even found an old oriental rug that I put in between the bookcases for the library area. Along with some old toss pillows it made a perfect reading nook. It was important to me that the room be a cozy welcoming place, as kindergarten is the introduction to school. Many of these children came from poor living conditions. I wanted them to see school as a safe and attractive environment. Finally, the room was complete.

Of course, the last thing to do was to fill it with people. During this school year the mandated student to teacher ratio changed to twenty to one. The lesser number of students worked well with the smaller room. I also had adult help. I had a couple wonderful parents who volunteered. Also, my daughter was in college nearby, training to be a teacher. She came in once a week and was great with the kids. I remember when we learned about letter K, she hopped into the room in a fur kangaroo costume with a pouch full of chocolate kisses to give out. My retired aunt, Gloria, came in once a week to work with small groups. I paid the two of them a little spending money. The district provided a daily aide. As my room was not actually attached to the playground, the aide would pick up my group and walk them to the kindergarten yard and supervise the outdoor time. He was a cheerful, strong young guy, who had completed training to become a highway patrolman and was on their waiting list to be hired. For the spring semester, I had a student teacher. Randy was completing his teaching credential requirements. He also was young and good looking. It was interesting that, with two single guys working in my room, the drop-in visits from young female teachers became quite frequent.

We did a big beach and ocean mural for open house. I filled the new bulletin boards with instructive material and with the children's colorful artwork. The room looked beautiful as well as being functional. The day after open house, all the classes marched through the whole school, and I overheard many comments that our room looked wonderful!

I felt like it functioned quite well as a kindergarten room, even though it had not been designed as such. Like any project that requires creativity, it was satisfying to take a dark, empty space and transform it. Room 11 was now a bright, cheerful environment for learning; a place to welcome little ones into their cozy home away from home.

My rocking chair

A colorful room 11

Daughter Dana helps

My student teacher Randy

Stories to Go

It was while I was working in Room 11 that I started a new program which I maintained for the rest of my teaching experience. The idea came about as a solution to a problem I had gradually become aware of.

Since I first started teaching, instruction in reading had always begun in the first grade. In kindergarten, I taught pre-reading skills such as letter recognition and phonics. Part of developing reading readiness is being read to each day. It was one of my favorite things to do. During story time each day I would read aloud and show the illustrations from beautiful picture books. Then I would ask comprehension questions and talk about such things as author, illustrator, title page and ending. Other times the children would select books from the classroom library and bring them to the rug to turn the pages and enjoy the pictures and "reading" time. I thought it was important for them to learn to value books and want to read before actually beginning.

With that in mind, I routinely reminded parents during conferences that the most important thing they could do to help their child progress was to read to them every night. Usually, they assured me that they would try to make it a habit. However, at Wilson I encountered many parents that had a problem with that. Poverty presented an obstacle. They did not own any children's books and they could not afford to buy them.

Of course, I immediately explained about the free books available at the public library. The negative responses surprised me until one of the moms explained it to me. "Oh no, *Maestra*, you have to have a library card," she almost whispered. She went on to explain that if you are worried about immigration status, you never fill out any paperwork with your name and address. "It is why we don't get a driver's license," she said. I didn't know how to respond to that unexpected information.

For some parents there was another obstacle. Even though the Costa Mesa Library was centrally located in the city it was not really close enough to be walking distance. Almost none of the parents owned a car. They mostly frequented businesses that were within a few blocks.

I began to ponder the problem. That year the local Kiwanis Club, a men's service organization started a new program. They filled the school multi-purpose room with new books that they had purchased. Each classroom teacher was allowed to choose fifty books to take back to their classroom to use however they wanted. I decided to start a take-home lending library.

The first thing I did was to photocopy the front of each book and glue that picture on the front of a sturdy manila envelope. Next, I ran those envelopes through the laminating machine, slit the top open with a razor blade and slipped each soft cover book into its matching envelope. Since the children could not yet read titles, they could easily select the story they wanted by the picture on the front of the envelope.

Then I laminated a second but slightly larger set of envelopes, one for each student, with their name on the front and instructions to the parent to read the story to their child and return it to school. Each child was given one of these large carry envelopes and was allowed to select one smaller envelope containing a book to place inside it to take home.

The next problem I encountered was language. Many of the parents could not read English. A few of the books were in Spanish, but the children could not read the titles to know which language the book was in. So, I put a red sticker on the corner of envelopes containing a book in Spanish and separated the books into two different boxes. I also bought more books in Spanish from Weekly Reader's inexpensive book club. Parents were very pleased to be able to read to their child in their language.

It was not long before the program was up and running smoothly. The main rule was that you could keep a book as long as you wished, but you could not exchange it for a new one until you returned both book and envelope. Most children chose to select a new book daily. The kids quickly settled into the routine. The first thing they did when they arrived at school was to hand me their full envelope and then select a new book, put it in the carry envelope and place it in their cubby ready to take home. It worked very well, and the children were being read to every night. I hope it gave them the knowledge that a book was something they could turn to for an exciting story, or one that made them laugh, or informed them about things like dinosaurs.

My goal was to instill a love of reading. I still remember my favorite time of the day as a young child. It was when my grandmother sat down in her big rocker, and I climbed up on her lap with a book. That was the moment she opened the front cover and said those magic words, "Once upon a time…"

Sean

I can clearly still picture a boy named Sean. One reason is because he was such a beautiful child. His hair, in need of a trim, was a shiny 14K pale gold. It curled down over big blue eyes that peeked through long dark lashes. His disposition was equally charming as he was always happy, enthusiastic, and sweet.

I had never met his parents, as five-year-old Sean lived with his grandmother, the adult who brought him to school. She was also the one who attended the parent conference. She brought along Sean's three-year-old little brother, whom she was also raising. He was equally beautiful with matching shiny gold curls. The brothers could easily have posed for cherubs in a Renaissance painting.

She told me that the mother was no longer in the picture, or able to care for the boys and their father was not around much. I commented on how lucky she was to have such beautiful grandsons live with her and be able to enjoy them. She looked at me like I was crazy and proceeded to tell me how tired she was and how active they were. She also complained about how hard it was to stretch her social security money to include them. "I just don't know how long I can keep them," she said in a very discouraged voice. (Meanwhile, I am thinking that anyone would adopt them in a heartbeat.) During the rest of the conference, I tried to encourage her by telling her how happy Sean was in kindergarten and how well he had adapted.

Not long after the conference, I was staying after school one afternoon. I had a habit of working late, as I enjoyed the quiet time in my classroom alone without interruptions. On this particular day I was working on the covered corridor outside my class, collecting the finger paintings I had left there to dry. I noticed a strange man walking toward me way across the deserted playground. My classroom was located around the corner and within sight of the office, which was deserted after 4:00. It was now past 5:00. Other teachers had long since gone home. I knew I was alone except for the night custodian, and I didn't see him around anywhere.

I am not usually a nervous person, but this guy looked strange, and he seemed to be heading right toward me. I thought of bolting for my classroom and closing the door. But I knew it didn't lock except from the outside with my key, which was back in the room in the depths of my purse. He was probably headed somewhere else, but I felt a frisson of fear. The man came closer. He was very thin and exceptionally tall, perhaps 6'6" or more. He wore a sleeveless undershirt, I guess to showcase his many tattoos. He had pierced ears with long greasy hair, which hung in stringy ringlets to his shoulders. His tattered jeans were barely held up, low on his hips by a wide leather belt. I felt intimidated. However, I stood my ground, although mentally poised to run.

He came straight toward me and asked in a low voice, "Are you Mrs. Munson?" When I nodded assent, he continued, "I'm Sean's daddy and I've come to meet his teacher."

You could have knocked me over with a feather, maybe one from the wings on which I was poised to fly. I never would have guessed this to be the father of the two beautiful cherubs. I invited him to come into the classroom and see some of Sean's work. He turned out to be very nice and was interested in Sean's progress. We held a good conference. Pleasantly surprised, I reminded myself not to judge a book by its cover.

Not long after that I again stayed late to change a bulletin board in my room. It was a large board that went from floor to ceiling. I always used it to showcase an ever-changing artistic display. First, I put up a roll of powder blue butcher paper for the sky and then a roll of grass that I had sponge painted in shades of green. We were about to begin a unit on the farm, so next I mounted a big red barn and a yellow haystack. Around it I stapled a wide variety of farm animals. It made a colorful and attractive mural, but I didn't stop there. I also liked to use my bulletin boards for instruction, so next to each object and animal I pinned a neatly printed label. I planned to pass out cards in class to the children. They could match their word to one on the wall and be able to 'read' their word out loud.

The board also served to motivate curiosity about the new unit. I liked to have it completed and surprise them when they arrived in the morning. The next day as the children arrived there was predictably a lot of interest in the new mural. Children love animals and there were chickens, chicks, sheep, horses, cows, pigs, lambs, and ducks everywhere. We sat on the rug below the picture and began to discuss the farm. They were excited as we named each animal. Many of the Spanish-speaking children were learning the English words for the first time. Sean was especially impressed with the cows and visibly excited. He kept waving his hand in the air, wildly anxious to get called on. "Sean," I said, finally giving him a turn.

"So that is a farm!" he said, as though a great mystery had at last been solved. "My daddy is at a farm. He has to be there for six months because he drank too much beer and was riding his motorcycle too fast." Hmm, the local correctional institute. A golden, happy Sean was smiling his angelic smile. I knew he was now picturing his daddy enjoying life among the sheep and the cows. Somehow, I couldn't bring myself to correct that impression.

Mariana

The month of October was always an enjoyable one. The children finally settled into a comfortable routine. I liked doing seasonal activities in that long uninterrupted month. The only holiday, Halloween, fortunately did not come until the last day, although five-year-olds always begin thinking about it on the very first day.

I tried to emphasize the time of harvest and signs of fall, rather than the approaching holiday celebration. Across the bulletin board that stretched the width of our room, I mounted sponge painted grass against a blue sky, a fitting background on which to pile our painted pumpkins. In their midst I placed a big colorful scarecrow. Following a lesson on crows, we made black paper crows and spread them across the mural sky.

The scarecrow was about the only scary thing in our room. I mostly avoided making things like monsters, goblins, ghosts, and witches. Of course, there were things that go bump in the night. We learned about nocturnal animals. I covered another board with black butcher paper to display our bats and owls. Black cats with springy tails strolled decoratively around the room.

Not only did we learn about crows, bats, and owls. We also studied spiders. I tried to point out how helpful they are in the garden. We watched a video of an orb spider laboriously constructing an intricate web. When it was complete and covered with dewdrops shining in the morning light, it was really quite beautiful. Although in real life spiders were something I always tried to avoid, they were the subject of one of my favorite art activities. On a sheet of manila paper, the children would each carefully draw a web with a black crayon. Then I would give them an orange and black spider sticker that they could affix to the web wherever they liked. Next, I would add a few drops of white glue over which they would sprinkle silver glitter. Mounted with orange paper framing them, the sparkling dew-covered spider webs made for a striking art bulletin board.

It seemed a good idea to avoid creating any scarier things than necessary. After all, I already had to include enough frightening activities in my curriculum. In fact, for my last few years at Wilson I was the school's disaster coordinator in charge of planning and scheduling disaster preparation. There were the usual fire drills to be held regularly, where it was necessary to explain to wide-eyed children, for the first time, that the loud clanging bells were just pretend, meant to teach us how to be safe if ever there were a real fire. There were also the earthquake drills, where I was responsible for creating scenarios for the response teams to deal with as the whole school filed out to the field. It was difficult to explain to the children about what to do during the initial shaking. They often were frightened as they huddled under the tables. I would hear the word *terramoto* said in a trembling voice. The hardest thing to explain to little ones was the new stranger drill where I would turn off the lights and lock the classroom doors and we would huddle quietly out of sight in case someone came on campus with a gun. It was a scenario that probably would never happen, safer to prepare for it but hard to avoid inspiring fear. Although new, this drill reminded me of the atomic bomb drills of my childhood, where we would duck and cover away from the windows imagining a mushroom shaped cloud over Los Angeles. Yes, we had scary stuff to deal with.

My personal frightening moment came one sunny October afternoon when the windows of the classroom stood open to allow the fresh air in. I was standing between the library bookshelf and the playhouse when two little girls came over pulling another girl between them. They began talking rapidly. The girl in the middle, a sweet shy girl named Mariana, was pale and frightened, tears were running down her cheeks. Their words were tumbling over each other, "Teacher, teacher, Mariana has a spider in her hair!" Their eyes were wide with alarm.

Their fear was contagious. Add to that, did I mention that spiders are my personal phobia. I am not afraid of snakes or dogs or bees or cockroaches, but spiders are a different story. They give me chills whenever I see one. I imagine the worst scenario, that it might somehow get on me and crawl across my skin. I looked at Mariana. I did not see any evidence of a spider. For the sake of the children, I told myself to remain calm. "I don't see it," I said.

"He is in her hair!" one of the girls almost screamed. Mariana was a pretty girl with the most beautiful head of hair, thick lustrous brown curls that tumbled in profusion all the way to her waist. Right now, she was shaking and appeared ready to faint. I know I was, as I imagined how she must feel.

"I think he might be gone now," I said hopefully, as I began searching through the beautiful curls. Suddenly, I saw it! It was probably the biggest spider I have ever encountered. He was orange and brown striped and had a huge bulbous shaped body. My heart began pounding. My skin broke out in goose bumps. Fighting an urge to run, I took a paperback book from the library shelf and managed to brush the spider onto the floor. Grabbing a plastic bowl from the playhouse sink, I quickly inverted it over the top of the spider and held it there. Every instinct I had was telling me to lift the bowl and step on it. But I hesitated to commit cold blooded spider murder in front of so many little witnesses gathered around. Besides, how would that fit in with the lesson about helpful spiders I had just taught?

Cautiously, I slid the thin paperback book between the bowl and the carpet. Then, holding tightly with every ounce of calm courage I could muster, I carried them over and held them out the open window and shook the spider out of the bowl. He dropped to the thick carpet of grass below and scurried beneath one of the many golden leaves that lay fallen and scattered about beneath the Sycamore tree. "Now he is back where he belongs," I said, "not in Mariana's curls!"

Finally, I could breathe again. I felt a sense of euphoria. I had not fled but had faced my worst fear with courage and had triumphed over my phobia. I remember little else about sweet little Mariana, only that one incident. I would like to think it taught me something about myself, for instance how I would react if ever the stranger drill became an unlikely reality. Hopefully, I would remain calm, face my fear, and do everything in my power to protect the precious little people in my care. There is nothing scarier than being responsible for their safety, not even monsters.

Arlene

To tell you about this memorable student, you need some background. In 1983, when my son was an active toddler, we were completing an addition to our house. I was so busy, that when a friend suggested I hire her cleaning lady, it sounded like a good idea.

That is how I met Sonya. She came to work on one day a week to do cleaning and ironing. She was efficient and helpful. We were both trying to improve our skill in another language. She would speak to me in English, and I would speak to her only in Spanish. The compromise worked well, with only an occasional hitch, as on the day I asked, "*Yo voy a la tienda, quieres algo?*" (To see if she wanted anything from the store.)

She nodded and replied, "Ahh hocks, please." When I didn't understand, she tried it louder. I finally told her in English that I didn't know that word, so I couldn't understand what she needed. Quite frustrated, she said loudly, "*Es Ingles!*" When I said it wasn't any English I knew, she reached under the sink, pulling out an almost empty blue carton with the familiar word AJAX on the side.

Oh, "Ahh Hocks," I shouted as the pronunciation light dawned on me. We had a good laugh together. That was the start of a friendship. I learned she had come to California from Guatemala. Gradually, she told me her immigration story. She had married young to a man from a well-known family. They had a son. Her husband was a successful attorney, but he was not faithful. She and the son left to live with her mother, but they had little to live on. Sonya wanted a better life. She made the painful decision to come to the United States leaving her son behind with her mother. The journey would be too difficult for a young child. Somehow, she managed to get the money to pay a coyote to smuggle her across the border from Mexico. She described the horror of crawling through the muddy filth of a sewer line, under the border, fearing discovery at any moment.

Here illegally, she got hired years ago by my friend as a nanny for their infant. Their little girl was in school now, so Sonya could take other jobs a few days a week, to earn extra money to send to Guatemala. My friend's home in Newport Beach was a beautiful one with a modern guest house where Sonya lived. With a fireplace and an ocean view, she had landed in a good spot.

While working for me, an amnesty program under President Reagan became available. My friend's husband, an attorney, helped Sonya with the paperwork to qualify and provided her with the necessary $500. Soon Sonya was legal.

She had been with me for a few years when she announced she had met a boyfriend. Not long after that came the news that she was pregnant, and that she had decided to keep the baby and move in with her boyfriend.

"Are you two going to get married?" I asked. She was adamant that they were not, although he wanted to. I was surprised at her decision. I had met Carlos, he was good-looking, a little younger than she was and was a friendly, easygoing person. He seemed like he would be a good husband and father, but she thought Hispanic men were not faithful in marriage and tended to dominate. She wanted to remain in charge of herself and her finances. As pregnancy advanced, she stopped working and moved in with Carlos, but would not marry him. I was sad to lose her services and so was my friend. When Sonya found out that her baby would be a girl, my mom crocheted a sweater, cap, and booties as a gift. I was about to begin substitute teaching and my schedule would be too erratic to allow me to hire help. We lost touch over the next few years.

At the beginning of the school year in 1995, I was teaching kindergarten and had just moved into my new classroom. One morning, a week after school had started, I looked up to see a lady enter the room, leading a pretty girl by the hand. I was startled when she smiled and said, "Hello, Mrs. Glenda." I recognized her. It was Sonya, after five years! I hugged her and she introduced her daughter, Arlene. I couldn't believe her baby was old enough for school. "I have come to put her in your class," she said.

I told her she would need to go to the office to enroll Arlene. Since I was in the middle of teaching, I didn't have time to explain that Wilson was now a bilingual school. Instruction in grades K-3 was given in a child's primary language. In kindergarten, both Eddy and Katie taught the Spanish speakers. My class was for English only or other languages that did not have large numbers at our school. Parents did not get to request a teacher. Despite Sonya's protests, the office placed Arlene in Eddy's class.

Days later, I received a call from the principal. She explained that both Sonya and Arlene were unhappy about the placement in Eddy's class. Sonya wanted Arlene in an English-speaking class but had been told that mine was already full. Arlene had spent hours crying every day, insisting that she did not want to go to school. Sonya had taken her to a doctor who wrote a letter. The crying was aggravating Arlene's asthma. The principal, said, "It would certainly make everybody happier if she were placed with you, but your class is full. You don't have to accept an extra student. I'll leave the decision up to you." I assured her that adding Arlene to my class would be fine with me.

Not only did Arlene not cry anymore, she was joyful! After all, she had gotten her way. She quickly became one of my favorite students. She was always enthusiastic, well behaved and did excellent work. Although Spanish was her first language, she spoke fluent English at school and seemed to prefer it, even on the playground. She made friends, learned easily and was a pleasure to have in my classroom.

Sonya was happy about Arlene's progress. She had tried to speak both languages to her as a young child and encouraged her English. In chatting with Sonya, I found out that she had studied, taken the test, and was now a naturalized United States citizen. She and Carlos were still together. Although they were not married, he was proving to be a very devoted father. Both worked hard. Sonya continued to send money to Guatemala to support her son, Favoricio.

Over the years that Arlene was at Wilson, she would stop in now and then to chat. When she was seven, she made the decision she wanted to have parents who were married, like her friends. Sonya told me that Arlene hounded them until Sonya finally gave in. She and Carlos were finally married, with a fiesta to celebrate. Arlene got her way, and happily boasted to me that she got to be the flower girl.

I saw Sonya occasionally, sometimes hiring her to work a party at my home. She met my mom (who had crocheted the baby clothes,) at one of these parties. Mom lived close by and hired Sonya to help her out one morning a week. I heard through her how Sonya and Arlene were doing. Sonya had succeeded in bringing a grown-up Favoricio legally into the United States, where he got a job. I sent a gift to Arlene when she graduated from high school. Carlos and Sonya not only worked days, but they started their own company cleaning industrial buildings at night. The last I heard from Arlene was a thank you note for a gift when she graduated from a local college. Carlos and Sonya were moving to Texas and buying a house close to a married Favoricio. Arlene was going too.

Of course, one of the reasons Arlene stands out in my memory is because of Sonya. But there is another reason. Sometimes, even at five years of age, a child has already developed a prominent character trait that stands out and will probably be with them throughout their life. In Arlene's case, that quality was determination. The first week I met her, she exhibited that trait, insisting on the class she wanted, speaking only the English language she preferred, later, convincing her parents to marry, achieving as a good student, and finally graduating from college. Her fierce determination had been apparent, even in kindergarten.

Paper Dolls

There was one project I frequently did for display at Open House. I began by passing out a cardboard pattern of a boy and a girl. The children would carefully trace the pattern with a pencil onto manila paper. Cutting it out was the next step and was a little difficult, but by spring most kindergarteners are getting proficient at using scissors and were able to do it slowly and carefully.

Next, they would color the hair, facial features, and shoes to make the doll resemble themselves. Back then, most paint stores carried a selection of wallpaper sample books which they would discard after a while. I had been given several of these old albums and the children would look through them to find patterns they liked and choose papers for dressing their dolls. I gave them cardboard patterns for dresses for the girls and shirt and pants for the boys. After they had traced and cut these out, they glued them on to their doll. Surprisingly the boys seemed to enjoy this activity just as much as the girls. For the last step they would sort through my tin of old buttons to choose those they wanted. With a hot glue gun, I would affix their choices to the shirts or dresses and their person was complete!

The art portion of their project was done, and the paper people surprisingly resembled the real ones. Next came the written part of the lesson. The children would sit with me and dictate information that I would write down. They would begin with, "My name is _____," then tell a little about themselves, such as their favorite thing to do, or if they had a pet, and then finish with what they would like to be when they grew up. They seemed to enjoy seeing their words being written down on a "talking bubble," like in a comic book. I would then mount their words next to their paper doll, usually around the perimeter of the room. They formed a colorful paper chain.

This art activity causes me to recall one particular little boy. I remember that after he finished, he brought his boy up to show me. He had done meticulous coloring, right down to carefully laboring to depict his sneakers. I recognized a probable future A student. I complimented him on his work, and he began to dictate, "My name is Andrew." I don't recall what he told next about himself, but if I had to recall something unique about this good student, I would have mentioned that at home he spoke Spanish with his mom and her family. When his parents conversed it was in English, so he was fluent in both languages. Yet, when his other grandmother was present, he spoke to her in Japanese so she would understand. I thought ability in three languages was something unique about him.

When I asked him what he would like to be when he grew up, he got very quiet and thoughtful. "Well," he said, "I think I might like to be a doctor, but does it take a long time?"

"Yes," I answered truthfully. "You have to stay in school for a lot of years but you like school a lot, don't you?"

He nodded yes. "But does it take a lot of graduations?" I laughed at his worried expression.

"Yes!" I replied, "After you graduate from kindergarten and elementary school, there is middle school and high school and college and medical school. That is a lot of graduations."

"Will you be there?" He asked, still worried.

"I tell you what, Andrew, if you keep having graduations and let me know, I will come and watch you." He seemed satisfied with that, and we wrote that he would like to be a doctor.

Weeks later, I watched him and all his classmates march around the playground in their paper mortarboards with crepe paper tassels and in due course I attended their fifth-grade graduation. I don't recall being made aware of middle school promotion ceremonies. However, years later I found out that Andrew's class was about to graduate high school. For some reason, I recalled my long ago promise and decided to attend.

I knew that interests change rapidly. All the would-be cowboys, firemen and astronauts and hopeful ballerinas, teachers, and movie stars probably had different goals by now. But I went anyway to Barnes and Noble and purchased a large colorful coffee table book on the anatomy of the human body, with transparency pages in the middle, showing bones, muscles, arteries etc. I wrapped it up and went to the graduation. Some names from that long-ago class from room 11 were recognizable, but not the faces. After the ceremony I asked around and finally located Andrew visiting with some of his friends. He remembered me, and I asked about his future plans. Did he intend to go on with school? I was pleased when he said he was enrolling at a local college. He seemed happy with the present and said it would come in useful as he was majoring in Biology!

I can still picture that row of paper dolls marching across the walls of my room. Of course, their creators grow and no longer resemble those little people. Their goals may or may not differ with time, but the one thing I hope never changes is that row of happy smiles!

Leave of Absence

The pathway of my teaching career was an unusual one. Unlike that of my cousin Sharon, hired after student teaching with me in her twenties. She stayed on at Ramona School, until retiring at age seventy. Also, my mother-in-law, Marion, spent thirty-five years teaching kindergarten in her Pasadena school. I thought that was the expected norm.

However, I began by teaching only one semester, stopping to have a baby. In the Fall, I was again employed in that district for three years while my husband finished medical school. I quit when we moved to Southern California for his internship. I was employed for the next three years in the Alhambra School District. Upon getting a divorce, I moved to the beach, where I got a contract with Newport Mesa School District. I remarried, and taught there for four years, before finally becoming a tenured teacher.

Once again pregnant, I took a year off on maternity leave. Wanting more time at home with my baby, I did not return to teaching when the leave was up. However, when my husband was diagnosed with a life- threatening cancer, I needed work. I was hired as a sub for the teacher who had taken my place and was taking a semester off for maternity. The following year, we teamed up and shared a contract. After that I returned to full-time teaching for the next couple of years. When my husband's health improved, once again I quit for childcare reasons while my daughter was in pre-school, thinking that I would come back when she was in school full day. Just as she was about to start a longer school day and I was ready to go back, I got pregnant with my third child and continued to stay at home. When he reached third grade, I finally was ready to return to work.

No jobs were available in my district, so I substituted for a year. The next year I was a long term sub all year for a teacher who was ill. The following year I was hired to fill a position that was classed as a long term sub all year. Finally, the following year I was given a contract and employed again in Newport-Mesa.

What a varied career! Over the course of the years, I had been employed by three different school districts, twice by the first one and three times by the third one. I had taught first grade and kindergarten and two classes of kindergarten a day for six years. Some years I had classrooms all to myself, but I had also shared classrooms with nine different teachers. I had done a shared contract and a maternity leave. For three and a half years I had been a substitute or a long-term substitute. At last, I thought my career path was done with interruptions, twists, and turns. My roller coaster career had finally settled down. I was mistaken.

My husband was unemployed and for months had been diligently searching for a job. One that he had been pursuing was now down to the final three candidates. It was for a position as a vice-president of a very large company. He returned from the last interview excited because he had been offered the job! The search was finally over. The only problem was the opportunity was in Texas. If he accepted, I would have to give up my job.

Moving to another state would be a huge change. We made a list of pros and cons. One of the most important negatives was leaving my job after going to so much effort to get rehired and all the work of fixing up room 11. There were more cons than pros on the list. It was one of the most difficult decisions I have ever made. I remember one day in class just standing there looking around at my classroom full of sweet children busily working and imagining leaving it all behind. But the deciding factor was that I loved my husband. This was such a wonderful opportunity for him. I agreed to go. My husband was ecstatic!

The plan was to stay in Texas for at least eight years until Duane retired. I did not expect to return to teaching (as by then I would be past retirement age.) Duane went ahead to Texas. I stayed behind and finished out the school year while he commuted on weekends and Dana finished getting her teaching credential. By June we were ready to move.

I thought I was closing the door on my career, however, one good thing about teaching is that it does offer alternatives and a variety of choices. Just in case things didn't go as planned, I filed an application for a leave of absence for the next year. I was surprised when it was approved.

It was so hard to say goodbye to my job and to California. We rented out our house in Newport and the new company had our belongings moved to our new home. It was a large hacienda in the Rio Grande valley. With fountains and a pool, it sat on a beautiful tree lined street with a stream and bridle trail behind it. Life in that Texas house proved to be fun. We swam in the pool, and I began remodeling and redecorating extensively. I loved the sound of hammering and the smell of sawdust, but there were days when I missed a classroom full of busy little people.

At the end of the next school year the district sent me a letter offering to extend my leave for another year. I was surprised, but on the side of caution I checked yes. That was a good thing, because toward the end of that summer my husband's job ended suddenly. We decided to return to California, sold the hacienda, and Duane's company provided a year of severance salary and paid for our move back.

The school year had already started when we arrived back at the end of September, so I stayed at home for the rest of my leave of absence to supervise the moving and settling in process. When the second year of leave was up, I let the district know I would be returning. A leave of absence means that when the leave is over you have a guaranteed job in the district, but not necessarily at the same grade level or school that you were at previously. I wondered where I would be placed.

As it turned out, when I left, my job had been filled by my student teacher, Randy. He had done excellent work in my classroom and was ready to obtain a job. However, while I was gone, things were reorganized, and kindergartens were again stacked. Randy wound up being placed in the same classroom with Eddy. He encountered the same resistance, but he ignored it. He had my desk moved into her room and reorganized the furniture so that one corner of the room made a little office for him and his teaching materials. Nevertheless, at the end of that year, he requested a change and was about to move to second grade. So, when my leave of absence was over, my principal requested me back at Wilson. Once again, I was about to share a room with Eddy!

The Bell Choir

Eddy and I were once again in the same classroom. She taught the morning kindergarten and I the afternoon class. After Randy, Eddy seemed resigned to having to share her room. We got along cordially because of our shared love of teaching. In December we were busy preparing for the upcoming holiday program. All four kindergarten classes were to participate. We decided on the songs each class would sing. Eddy would accompany on the piano. I would stand in front and direct and the other two kindergarten teachers would shepherd the classes on and off the stage.

We had everything carefully planned, until Eddy had another idea. In addition to their singing songs, she wanted to choose children from our two classes to play the tone bells. I had never had the opportunity to use them before, but Eddy was familiar with them. She got out the set that was stored in our classroom and proceeded to demonstrate. The bells were large and colorful with wooden handles. She chose a few students and handed each one a different colored bell. Then she placed a series of cards with colored circles into a pocket chart. As she used a pointer to indicate each circle, a child would play the bell of the corresponding color and suddenly we were hearing the song, Jingle Bells. I thought the bell number was creative and agreed it would be a nice addition to our program. We both began to practice the number with our classes.

The children became very good at playing the bells. The problem arose when we marched the classes over to the multipurpose room to practice. There were no windows in the big room and the lighting was poor. In the dimness the children could not see the circles well enough to distinguish between the similar green and blue or red and orange. They played the wrong bells! I was hesitant to direct them if they were going to make mistakes and I told Eddy we shouldn't include that number. It could sound awful. Eddy disagreed. "They'll be fine," she said, and volunteered to direct them. Her opinion prevailed, and we kept the bell number in the printed program. We continued to practice.

The morning of the final rehearsal arrived. For some reason, Eddy did not show up for work. She had not called for a sub. The other morning teacher and I took our classes over to rehearse as planned. We mostly practiced getting the kids on and off the stage because, without Eddy, we had no piano accompaniment.

We were almost ready to leave to go back to our classrooms when I looked up to see Eddy walk in. She was very late to work! She looked frazzled and explained that she had been in an auto accident on her way to school. "Oh no!" I exclaimed. "What happened?"

She looked a bit confused, "I'm not sure," she said. "I think it may have been my fault. "The other driver and I were not injured but the cars are quite damaged."

"Well, the important thing is that you are O.K.," I said. "Cars can be fixed." I told her that we were about to leave but asked her if she wanted us to stay so she could play the piano for us.

She hesitated but shook her head, "No, they'll be fine," she answered.

She glanced at the piano and whispered something odd, "I think I forget how." I guessed she must still be in a bit of shock from the accident

The following day was the holiday program. I arrived at school early. The multipurpose room was filled with rows of chairs for the audience. Printed programs were stacked in readiness. In the classroom bright red paper Santa hats were lined up awaiting the children. Everything was in order until the phone rang. The office was calling to inform me that Eddy had called in sick and that a sub was on the way. Would I please guide her in whatever she needed to know to get Eddy's class through their performance. I glanced up at the clock. I had five minutes before forty children arrived in the room, as both classes would be coming together on a morning schedule for the program.

I felt a minute of mild panic. The program was likely going to be a disaster, with no one to play the piano or lead the tricky bell choir. I didn't have time to worry about it. The sub walked in and wanted to know what she should do. I filled her in on the schedule and set her to work taking role and costuming the children in their hats and jingle bell necklaces as they arrived. I left her in charge and began to search the school for the music teacher who was on campus to accompany the upper grades. I located her in a fifth-grade class and asked if she could please play the piano for our kindergarten songs. She agreed but said I would have to provide her with sheet music. After some frantic searching, I managed to locate music. I hurried back to the classroom. The children were costumed and ready but there was no time left. I would just have to direct the bell number myself and hope. I quickly lined the children up, grabbed the box of bells and the pocket chart, and away we went to the multipurpose room. The rosy cheeked children in their Santa hats all sang beautifully, accompanied by the music teacher on the piano. Somehow the program went perfectly, even the bell choir performed in the dim light. They must have memorized which circle was their cue!

After school I telephoned Eddy as I was sure she would be worried about her absence. When I told her how well it went, she just said, "Oh." I asked if she would be back tomorrow, the last day before vacation and the day of the class parties. "No, I still have a headache from the stress of the accident." I asked if she wanted me to stuff the paper stockings her class had made with the candy canes I saw on her desk and distribute them, but she just wanted to get off the phone. I was confused because it was very unlike her to be disinterested. Perhaps she was disoriented from the crash.

When we returned to school after the new year, we learned that Eddy was still not feeling well enough to come in. I heard she was having some tests done. The district hired a sub. After a while we were told that Eddy would not be returning for the rest of the school year! She was currently in a convalescent care facility. One afternoon I went to visit her with the other kindergarten teachers. She seemed glad to see us and liked the cards her class had made. She was interested to hear how they were doing. She did not seem to be in pain but confided that the doctors had diagnosed a brain tumor. She was vague about what treatment options were available. I hoped they could remove the tumor with surgery. The sub continued to teach Eddy's class and the rest of the school year seemed to fly by. We received occasional updates on how she was doing. It made me sad to think how she must miss school, as teaching was her life. She was too young to retire.

Many people are not aware that kindergarten is a separate department from other grades. After kindergarten, the next graduation you may hold (rather than a promotion) is upon completion of high school. In an area where the dropout rate is high, kindergarten is possibly the only graduation some students ever experience. So, our graduation ceremony was a big deal.

When the June day arrived, the girls were all dressed in shiny patent leather shoes and lace dresses. The boys wore suits and ties. With smiles on their faces and construction paper hats with crepe paper tassels, they were ready to accept their colorful diplomas from the principal. The crowd of happy parents sat in chairs on the blacktop as they proudly watched the graduates march around the playground to the strains of Elgar's Pomp and Circumstance. As I watched, it brought a lump to my throat. Actual tears came later when we heard that Eddy had died just as the ceremony ended. She was in a coma and couldn't have been aware, but the timing was so coincidental. It was like she was waiting for her last class to graduate. I think she somehow realized her job of teaching them was finished. She could rest. As with the bell choir she had prepared so well, she knew that, even without her, the children would be fine. The music would still go on.

Nora

Occasionally I had students in my class who came from homes where they were neglected. Nora was one of those children. She enrolled after the beginning of the school year, as she had just moved into the school attendance area.

She was very cute and looked a little like Orphan Annie with her mop of red gold curls, pale skin and a scattering of freckles across her nose. She was very likeable and always peppy and smiling. She usually wore wildly unmatched pants and tops as though she dressed herself. I first noticed this apparent lack of supervision when she arrived at school one cold rainy day wearing a sleeveless sundress and rubber flip flops. I sent her to the nurse to get a sweater from the school's supply of extra clothing.

After school each day she would sit and wait for someone to come and pick her up. Often it was a brother that came to walk her home. Sometimes it was an adult in a car. Frequently they were late. One day no one showed up. After delaying thirty minutes I took her over to the office and let her wait in a chair.

I looked up her emergency card and called her home phone number. I thought surely someone at home must be very worried about her by now. The phone rang several times and eventually a woman answered. "Is this Mrs. _____? "I asked.

"Yeah, who's this?" she asked in a slurred voice.

"This is Nora's kindergarten teacher."

There was a long silence and then, "Oh, what do you want?"

"Well, her class got out thirty minutes ago and no one has come to pick her up yet." I was waiting for her to apologize and say something like she didn't notice the time.

Instead she surprised me with, "Well I can't get her, I'm taking a nap now," she said in an unconcerned woozy voice. I guessed she was probably in no shape to drive from alcohol or maybe drugs.

She didn't sound at all worried about retrieving her child. "Well someone needs to come and pick her up right away," I said in a firm loud voice as she seemed like she might be about to hang up and go back to sleep. "She is waiting in the office."

"O.K." she said. "I'll try to find her brother," and she slammed the receiver down. A brother arrived a few minutes later to walk Nora home. She happily skipped away with him.

The federal government provided a healthy snack for the kindergarten children, which they had every day at the beginning of recess. However, the Thanksgiving holiday was approaching and I was planning a special treat for the day before our vacation. We would create a party in our room. To celebrate the first Thanksgiving, we would make turkey soup and a trail mix to go with it. A few days before the event I sent home a note to the parents listing the ingredients that we would need, if they cared to contribute one. Some children brought in fresh carrots, a bunch of celery, dried noodles, and cans of chicken broth for the soup. I planned to bring seasonings and a turkey chub to dice up. For the trail mix they contributed packages of: cheese-its, peanuts, candy corn, cereal, raisins and pretzels. Some children didn't bring anything, and I assured them that was fine, but Nora looked a little sad about it.

The next day at recess time she tugged on my shirt. "Teacher, teacher, I have something to show you." She pulled me over to her cubby and drew out an old tin lunch pail. She was excited as she opened it to show me the contents. "I brought something for the feast!" Her little face was beaming with pride.

I peered into the beat-up lunch pail and was shocked at the contents. Inside were three unwrapped slices of bread. They were all partially covered with a layer of blue mold. I looked at Nora and her delighted smile. "Why thank you honey. That is so nice of you to bring something to share."

"I know," she said and skipped outside to recess.

The day of the party the children set the classroom tables with the placemats they had colored and fringed and the colorful turkey napkins and plastic soup bowls and spoons I had bought. I turned on my big electric crock pot and we began to add ingredients: cans of chicken broth, diced turkey, chopped celery, sliced carrots, dried noodles and seasonings. In a huge plastic salad bowl, we assembled the peanuts, raisins, cereal, pretzels, and candy corn and took turns stirring the trail mix. Then I scooped it into the cute turkey nut cups we had made from small milk cartons. While the soup cooked, the children put on the costumes they had made. Some wore pilgrim hats and others feathered Indian headbands. Nora looked adorable with her red gold curls peeking out from under a white pilgrim bonnet tied under her chin. We celebrated with Indian dances and Thanksgiving poems and songs. The delicious aroma of hot turkey soup filled the room. When our feast was ready, the soup was ladled into bowls and the punch poured. The class settled themselves at the festive table. Indians sat side by side with pilgrims and all declared it to be good soup and a delicious feast was enjoyed by all. Nora never even noticed the absence of bread or perhaps she thought it was in the soup.

On another day, worried about her nutrition, I casually asked her what kinds of things she usually ate for dinner. "What's dinner?" she asked, looking puzzled.

Maybe they call it something else I thought. "Well it's the food you eat at night time, after school is over, but before you get ready for bed. "Does your mom cook you something then?" I asked.

She thought hard for a minute. "No, she doesn't do that," she shook her curls. "But sometimes my brother fixes me a bowl of cereal or maybe peanut butter. Is that dinner?"

I don't remember exactly how the referral occurred, but early that spring Nora was withdrawn from school. Social Services had removed Nora and her brothers from their home and sent them to a county facility. I was told that an investigation revealed that there was no adult in the house when the children got home from school. The garage door to the alley had been chained so that it would only open about a foot. The kids would get inside by lying on the ground and rolling under it.

I was never told the outcome of the legal proceedings, but I assumed that in the future improved home conditions would be mandated and supervised or the children would be placed in foster care.

Sometimes, especially during Thanksgiving dinner, I can't help but remember a cute little pilgrim girl named Nora, enjoying her soup. I can still see the glowing pride she showed upon offering the only food she had; three slices of moldy blue bread.

Off We Go

There is one aspect of teaching that I haven't mentioned, that of field trips. They did not occur often, but they provided some memorable days. In my first job in South San Francisco, I don't recall taking any kindergarten trips. Perhaps funding for the buses did not start until first grade.

In Alhambra we were allowed to take one trip each year. Our first excursion was to Travel Town in Griffith Park. The other teacher and I loaded both our classes and some parent volunteers onto the bus. This was an experience in itself, as many children had never ridden one. Part of Travel Town was an assortment of huge train engines and railroad cars parked on tracks. Our kindergartners swarmed around and over them like so many ants. It was impossible to keep an eye on all of them at once. Thank goodness for the parents who were helping. Fortunately, when we lined up to board the bus to leave, both stressed out teachers did a careful head count and, miraculously, we each had the same thirty-five children we had arrived with.

The next year we decided to leave Travel Town to the first grades as their unit was transportation. Instead, we went to the Los Angeles Zoo. I decided to make construction paper nametags of bright yellow and affixed them to the kids' shirts with a safety pin. This would make my group easily identifiable. The thing is, I didn't anticipate the goats. When we went into the petting zoo area, the goats began to jump up on the children. They greedily gobbled up every one of the paper nametags! At least they didn't eat the safety pins.

When I moved to the Newport-Mesa School District, I found out there was a small zoo at Prentice Park in Santa Ana. It had a lot fewer animals than the L.A. Zoo but provided an interesting outing. There were lots of birds and monkeys and some big cats. The best part was a petting yard where the children could go in with the animals. It even had some giant Galapagos tortoises there as big as the kids, (a few years later they were removed from the zoo.) Having learned a bit from earlier field trips, this time I did not rely on nametags only. I tied a bow of bright colored roving yarn around each child's wrist. The other teacher did the same thing in a different color. The kids were told to stay with the red group or yellow group. It greatly facilitated sorting the classes when it was time to leave. It was a good thing I did that, because as we were walking around the zoo, I happened to look up just in time to spot a red bow at the back of another class walking by us in another direction. I couldn't read the name tag from a distance but, sure enough, the bow was on my little Alfonzo, a babyish non-English speaking boy in my class. He was dutifully shuffling along behind a line of kids that had just passed us. The teacher was loudly announcing in Spanish that everyone should follow her. Alfonzo was complying and was on his way back to a preschool in Santa Ana if I hadn't seen the bow.

Sometimes it was not a bus trip. One day we walked to the nearby fire station. The only indigenous life forms we saw there were some very good-looking young firemen who greatly interested our pretty student teachers. The kids enjoyed a turn to put on a fireman jacket and helmet.

The next year we went to Lion Country Safari, a wild animal theme park nearby. It was amazing. The wild animals roamed the grassy area while we stayed within the confines of the slowly moving bus as we drove through the park. We saw all sorts of wildlife, including lions, up close to the bus. Hippos waded in water nearby. After the tour was over, a show was presented in part of the park where the kids sat on bleachers.

One detail I remember is that, for the occasion, I sewed a pants suit of synthetic cheetah fur to wear. I fit right in.

After I took a time out for maternity leave, I returned as a substitute teacher. One day (as recounted elsewhere) I reported to a job to find out that in fifteen minutes I would be taking the class on a field trip. It turned out to be a cruise of Newport Harbor. I had just time to tie bows, but since the children were strangers it left me calling out things like, "Hey, girl in the red sweater, stop leaning over the side of the boat!" I was sure I was going to have to dive in.

Sometimes trips were prearranged by the district. We went to the performing arts center for a tour and *Peter and the Wolf.* Also, every year the drama department at Newport Harbor High School put on a holiday performance for the kids. It was so well organized. The drama students in costumes met the bus and ushered us into the auditorium. The plays were cute. Everyone had fun and the kids were given candy canes and escorted back to the buses.

When I was at Wilson School, some trips were within walking distance, so they were free. One day we visited the fields behind nearby Estancia High School and rode on the model train there. Another time, on a blustery March Day, we walked again to the same fields. A tradition of the teacher next door to me, this day each child brought their own kite from home. Even though I grew up loving to fly kites, (and we got many of them up,) with forty kites there were some torn kites or tangled strings with impossible knots at the end of the day. I decided not to do that again. Another trip I decided never to repeat, with that same teacher, was to the ice-skating rink. It was too time consuming to lace up skates on everyone. Almost all the kids could not skate and were slipping, sliding, and falling in every direction. I spent the whole time trying to teach them how to ice skate without landing on my own backside!

A field trip was useful as the culmination of a social studies unit. Since we often did the farm as our unit for Open House, several times repeating a trip to the farm at the Orange County Fairground. There was a guide provided who would give us a tour. First the children would see the gardens, where large cucumbers, melons and pumpkins fascinated these apartment dwellers. Next, we would visit the small animals' area, a favorite with the children. One time we saw a whole litter of adorable piglets just hours old. There was a newborn calf and other baby animals, colorful chickens, and rabbits. The kids could go in the petting area and cuddle the sheep and goats. Finally, we ate lunch at the picnic tables, a pleasant way to end our visit.

My very favorite field trip was also repeated several times, and one that I got down to a system. When our unit was the ocean, we would culminate with a trip to the beach. The children would arrive wearing swimsuits and bringing towels and dry clothes. I bought a colorful pail and shovel for each child and used a paint pen to print names on the front. The cafeteria supplied a picnic lunch and juice packets to place in each pail. The bus took us to the beach at the Newport Beach Harbor Department. It was perfect for supervising the kids. Even though it had a large area of sand, the strip of bay at the front was quite narrow. I could keep my eyes on anyone in the water and most importantly, it had no waves. There was a jetty with rock crabs and, on the other side of the breakwater, lots of boats going by. We hunted buried pirate treasure from a map I made, to uncover a chest of gold-covered chocolate coins. We ate our picnics on the towels and then the kids happily built sandcastles, hunted for shells, and caught rock crabs. There were convenient restrooms with showers when it was time to clean up for the bus. They could keep any shells or treasure they found but I insisted on no crabs for the return trip!

A very touching moment occurred on one field trip to the beach. Even though Costa Mesa is only a fifteen-minute drive to the ocean most of these children had never been to the beach. Most families did not own a car but walked to the Spanish speaking stores in the neighborhood. This trip was going to be a first. As the bus full of excited children drove along, one child could not contain his joy and began to chant, "We're going to the beach!" One voice after another picked up the refrain until the whole bus was chanting over and over, "We're going to the beach!" It brought tears to my eyes. There is more than one way to teach. You can read books about the beach or show pictures, but these kids were about to feel the sand between their toes, splash in the bay, watch boats go by, or catch a crab. I was privileged to help them take a first step into the big world beyond kindergarten. I could experience, through their eyes, the thrill of seeing things for the first time, all through the magic carpet of a field trip.

Off on our field trip to the beach!

Down the Chimney

It was the day of another year's holiday program. My kindergarten class was ready. They had been practicing for weeks, since Thanksgiving in fact. Today was their big day. It was time to perform on the school's stage.

As their teacher, I was both excited and nervous. I hoped all our practice would result in a good performance. In our classroom, the aide helped me to costume the children in their Santa hats. Made of red crepe paper with a white paper cuff and tassel, they made the children look festive and accentuated their adorable rosy cheeks. They also wore a necklace of yarn with a giant jingle bell around their neck. It was to be used when they sang Jingle Bells, but it also created a merry tinkling as I marched them all in a line over to the multi-purpose room.

The huge room was filled with parents who came to see their little ones perform. I looked over to see that my husband, Duane, was also there in the front row. He smiled and waved. Currently retired, he was available to come and join the audience. I led the children up onto the stage and arranged them in neat rows on the risers. Then I went down the steps and returned to stand on the floor of the auditorium directly in front of the stage. The other kindergarten teacher walked her class to the stage and came down to seat herself at the piano. She would accompany us and I would direct both classes.

Usually we sang at least four songs, one in Spanish, as all the children were bilingual. This year our program would conclude with their favorite, a song about Santa, "Up on The Housetop". The song has cute motions that go along with the words.

Duane had visited my class one day while we were practicing. As I taught the motions, he laughed when he heard me explaining that Santa was *muy gordo* and how he wiggled his hips to get his very fat tummy down the chimney. Later, when I asked if he wanted to attend the program he said, "Are you kidding? I wouldn't miss a chance to sit out in the audience and watch you wiggle down the chimney."

I am not very musical, but over the years I learned that the secret to successfully directing kindergartners is to get them to constantly keep their eyes on you. Otherwise they all start at different times or forget the words or motions or stand transfixed at the sight of the audience.

At last we were ready to begin. The lights dimmed, the crowd hushed and the children began to sing. Amazingly they all stayed together as they belted out the words to their four songs. Even though it was long they seemed most comfortable with the Spanish song, "*El Arbol de Navidad*." Finally, we concluded with "Up on The Housetop".

The words rang out,

Up on the housetop reindeer pause,

Out jumps good old Santa Claus.

(The children smiled as they spread their hands out)

Down through the chimney with lots of toys

All for the little ones Christmas joys.

(They did the cute hip wiggle as they knelt down.)

Ho, Ho, Ho, who wouldn't go?

Ho, Ho, Ho, who wouldn't go?

(Their hands pantomimed Santa's fat belly.)

Up on the housetop, click, click, click, ...

(They snapped their fingers.)

And down thru the chimney with old St. Nick.

I directed the motions and went down the chimney in my tight red dress, imagining Duane watching from the front row. The children took their bows to thunderous applause.

I climbed back up the five steep steps to the stage and supervised as the kids carefully got down off the risers, then joined the line across the front of the stage. I began walking slowly backwards and they followed me like baby ducks in a row. I was thinking about how well they were doing as I took the next step backward, onto, - nothing but air! I had reached the stairs sooner than I thought.

Startled, I grabbed for the stair rail. There wasn't one! Arms flailing, I began falling backwards. My right toe touched a step but slipped off the edge of it. I tried to correct in midair by leaning forward. I continued falling. My left foot encountered another step. With an instinctive reaction I pushed off hard. That caused me to spring upwards and back and somehow, I landed with bent knees and both feet together on the floor at the base of the stairs. Stunned, I regained my balance, my smile and composure, and kept walking backwards as though nothing had happened. I motioned to the children to stay in line. They were gawking at me but they followed.

Meanwhile Duane had leaped from his front row seat to rush over to me. "Are you, all right?" he asked. "Everyone thought you were going down!" I nodded that I was fine, but I glanced behind me. There was the sharp corner of the piano that I would likely have struck if I had fallen backwards. The fact that I wasn't hurt was a Christmas miracle.

A couple other parents came over to inquire if I was all right. One of the dads jokingly said, "I'd give you a ten on your gymnastics performance. You even stuck the landing!"

Back in the classroom, as I conducted the class Christmas party, I repeated that remark to Duane. He grinned and said, "Yeah, it was amazing, even better than watching you go down the chimney!"

Daisy

Open House was always my favorite event on the teaching calendar. It usually was held in May, near the end of the school year. It was the perfect time to showcase the children's work and was an opportunity for parents to see the growth and progress of their child.

I always chose a theme for the couple months of instruction leading up to Open House, centering activities around that. Over the years I had done many different themes: spring, circus, dinosaurs, space, Mexico, zoo, transportation, "It's a Small World", the farm and the ocean. Some of these I repeated several times.

When I finally moved back into the large kindergarten room at Wilson, I did not need to share it with another class. I was delighted with all the space afforded for Open House. I chose ocean as a theme as we were located nearby. There was a big bulletin board that extended across the entire front of the room. It was perfect for a huge mural filled with sea creatures made by the children. I filled the rest of the many bulletin boards around the room with their theme related artwork and stories. Colorful sea life they had painted, and stuffed fish hung suspended from the ceiling, even the windows displayed their watercolors of undersea life. The library table held books that the class had written together. One wall held photos of each child on our field trip to the beach.

Also displayed on the tables was my favorite project. For several years now, I had assembled a kindergarten yearbook for each child. The size of a large sheet of construction paper, it contained a couple pages for each month of the school year. It held samples of seasonal art projects, some words to songs or poems they had learned, self-portraits, handprints, writing samples, stories they wrote and their photo on the front. All the pages were laminated, punched, and assembled on notebook rings. It was a lot of work but formed a permanent keepsake.

When preparation was done, the room was so clean it sparkled. My husband sent a bouquet of flowers for my desk, a reward for the many extra hours of staying late after school to get the room ready. It was always worth it at Open House to see how proud the kids were of our room and their work. They enjoyed showing it off to their parents. Of course, the resulting praise they received bolstered their self-confidence and interest in learning.

Early in my teaching career I had learned the hard way that some parents don't bother to take the time to attend Open House. Sometimes only half of them would show up, which I found very disappointing after all that preparation. Over the years I got wiser. I no longer depended on just the notes from the office to inform parents of the event. I sent home a separate letter to the parents in both English and Spanish. I also had the children make a colorful invitation to take home. I told them they could ask their parents and even grandparents to come. But since dates can easily be forgotten, or notes can remain unread in the bottom of backpacks, I came up with yet another reminder. On the day of Open House, the children went home from school wearing a colorful headband announcing Open House tonight! Right in front of their face, it was impossible to ignore! I usually received a 100% turnout.

On the morning after Open House, I was still thrilled with the good attendance at the successful event of the previous night. Although I had a sign-in sheet out for the parents, I didn't have to check it to know who had attended. I could see at a glance if any child's yearbook was still left. There was only one yearbook remaining on the table. I glanced down at the photo on the cover, the smiling face of Daisy.

I thought I could fix that. I knew Daisy lived with her aunt who usually picked her up from school. That afternoon I waited with Daisy on the bench outside my door. After all the other children had left, a car finally pulled up on the street in front of our playground. The driver honked and kept the engine running. "That's my aunt," said Daisy and started to jump up.

"Stay there" I told her and walked out to the street. I told her aunt that she was the only one to have missed our wonderful open house and that Daisy was so excited to show her all her work and I invited her in. It took a lot of convincing, as she said she was tired, but finally she parked the car and accompanied me into the classroom, none too happy about it.

An overjoyed Daisy began to show her around our room. Her aunt had told me at a conference that she had custody because Daisy's mom was currently in prison. The father was no longer in the picture. There had been a little brother too, an infant, but he was put up for adoption. "I couldn't take him too," she had said, "drug babies are too fussy. Besides, even one kid is a lot of trouble." She had agreed to take Daisy and to "see how it went."

The aunt and Daisy arrived at the writing center. I listened as Daisy excitedly continued the tour. "This is the word wall, and these boxes have words with pictures next to them, see, so you know what they spell. You can use them to write a story. This is my mine about a fish." She smiled proudly. Her aunt nodded. They wandered around the room with Daisy continuing to babble, trying her best to interest her aunt and show off her accomplishments to please her. When they had completed their circuit, I gave the yearbook to her aunt. She flipped through it quickly.

"O.K. let's go now Daisy. I need to get my nap," she said in a tired voice.

I thanked her nicely for taking the time to come in. I watched as she trudged across the playground to her car with Daisy skipping along beside her. "At least Daisy is happy," I thought.

The following year, I was in the lunchroom with the first-grade teacher when she related something that had happened in her class that day. "I was about to introduce a lesson on vowels, and I asked if anyone knew what they were," she said. "Usually no one knows, but one of your last year's kids answered."

She called out, "Yes, Mrs. Munson told us all about them!" Then she stood up and started singing to the tune of Bingo: "I know a song about the vowels, and I can sing it to you. A E I O U, A E I O U…"

"Who was it?" I asked.

"Daisy," she said.

I laughed, "Yes, she is enthusiastic about learning."

A few weeks later when I inquired about Daisy, her teacher said she was no longer in our school. "She is in foster care now and is being put up for adoption. Her aunt no longer wanted to raise her."

I felt sorry for Daisy. The thing she worried about had finally happened. She was being given away, despite trying so hard to please. I wondered about her chances of being adopted. Probably most people want a baby, not a six-year-old.

Sometimes I wonder what makes the memory of one child stand out in my mind. Every child is precious and unique, but some leave a more indelible impression. They leave you wondering how their future will turn out. Perhaps it is how they deal with difficult circumstances so early in their lives. The memory of this girl reminds me of an afternoon on my patio when I looked down to notice a little miracle. A small green plant had sprouted up in a narrow crack in the cement. There was no soil around it. At first, I thought it was a weed, but as days went by, it continued to grow and finally bloomed into a pretty flower. I marveled at its persistence. How had that little seed found a home in such a tiny crack in an otherwise impenetrable surface? How did it continue to grow with no visible means of nourishment? How did it not wilt from thirst, surrounded as it was by a desert of concrete? Somehow, it survived. It even thrived, turning its cheerful face always toward the bright sunlight. **That hardy flower was a daisy**!

A few weeks later I found out that Daisy was being adopted by a nice young couple.

Alena

Some memories are frustrating. For the sake of privacy, let's call her Alena. It was something she said that first alerted me. I had been standing nearby the table where she was coloring and talking with two other children. I had not really been paying attention to their conversation, but I overheard a partial remark that made me question.

"Honey, what did you just say?" Try as I might I could not get her to repeat it. In fact, she looked at me with this look of guilt like she had said something she shouldn't have. She not only wouldn't repeat her remark but clamped her lips closed and wouldn't say anything. That was very unlike Alena who normally was a Chatty Cathy who never stopped talking. It was that look that set off an alarm for me.

I hadn't heard exactly what she had said to the boys at her table, but I thought it was something like "and sometimes they hold you like this" and she demonstrated with her arms clamped tight to her sides like she was being restrained. I thought I glimpsed a momentary shiver of fear but, like I said, questions got me nowhere.

Maybe I had not heard the snippet of conversation correctly and was misinterpreting her look. I second guessed myself but decided to investigate a little anyway. I knew Alena rode the bus home each day, but I didn't know about after school supervision. I asked her, "Who is there to watch you when you get home every day? Is it Mom or Dad?"

Her answer was not reassuring. "No, they are at work. My uncle is there." That left me feeling a little uneasy, perhaps imagining a threat that wasn't there.

In the days that followed I kept a close eye on Alena. She had always been a very happy outgoing child. I noticed lately that she was being a little disruptive on occasion, unlike her usual behavior. One day when we were out at recess, two little girls came running up to me to tattle on Alena. "Teacher, Alena is in the playhouse, and she is taking down her panties and showing the boys! She shouldn't be doing that should she?" Their words tumbled out and they were obviously horrified.

"No," I said, "I'll take care of her," and I marched across the yard. The playhouse was a sturdy wooden house that had been donated to the school. It was set back in an isolated corner of the yard underneath the shade of an enormous Ficus tree. The little shuttered windows were permanently fixed open, which is how the girls had peeked in. Alena was still inside along with a couple of somewhat disinterested boys. I shooed them out and had a little talk with Alena about how inappropriate her behavior was.

I now knew there was definitely a problem. It was no longer just suspicion. I had by this time taught over a thousand kindergartners and never encountered this behavior before. Although occasional little boys might drop their jeans to urinate outside or compare equipment, Alena's behavior was outside the scope of normal.

I went to my principal. We discussed my suspicions, and she agreed that I had cause to be concerned, but that there was nothing concrete to report to social services. She suggested we do a home welfare visit together. We went to the apartments where Alena lived with her parents. It was an older stucco building set far back on the lot. In place of a lawn there was an expanse of knee-high brown weeds. The mom let us in and spoke to us in Spanish. The open unmade hide-a-bed sofa took up almost all the space in the tiny living area, leaving no room for a child to play indoors. We talked cordially for a while with the mom. We were told that she and the father often worked and when they did, the neighbor man watched Alena. We also learned that he was not actually a relation, but a family friend that Alena just called "uncle." As we left, I noticed that the unit that the "uncle" lived in was part of a row of boarded-up garages that had been turned into rooms for rent. There were no windows or doors on the front side of them. For me it was yet another red flag.

I recalled that Alena's behavior had altered a couple of months ago. It was not long after an incident where she had an upset stomach at school and soiled her clothing. The uncle had come to school to take her home. A bath would have been in order, and maybe that was the start of something. The timing coincided. It was another piece of the puzzle to consider.

The principal and I decided we needed to have a conference with the parents to discuss Alena's behavior and to alert them that it was possibly a warning sign. The principal needed to be in on the conference for several reasons, one being that although Alena was completely fluent in English, the parents spoke only Spanish. I knew my Spanish was not up to a conference that concerned such a delicate subject. My principal could be both a translator and a witness. We held a long conference with the parents and told them of Alena's behavior and our concerns. Without making any accusations we emphasized that to be on the safe side she should not be left alone with the neighbor. Summer vacation was just about to start, and we told them that one of them should stay home to supervise her and always keep her within sight. They nodded and agreed they would arrange their work schedules, but I got the feeling that they thought we were being alarmists and resented the inference about their friend.

Without any concrete proof, we didn't feel we could report anything to county social services. Summer arrived, but I was left with a lot of uncertainty, and I worried about Alena. I could only hope her parents had heeded our advice and were being the only adults to watch her over the summer. At this point I felt helpless. I was torn between thinking I was being overly suspicious and a feeling of responsibility to protect my student.

The next year when Alena was in the first grade, I received a call from the school nurse. She wanted to know what had triggered my suspicions of sexual abuse about Alena last year. I related to her that it was nothing definite, just my uneasy feelings that kept growing. I related about the overheard partial remark, the reticence to answer, the playhouse incident, the supervision by the "uncle" and the set up at the apartments. "It was mostly just intuition. Why are you wanting to know?" I asked.

She told me that she and the principal were in the process of submitting a report to social services. "Since you are no longer her teacher, I can't explain more in the interest of privacy, but I can tell you that she has the kind of infection that a little girl should not have."

Thematic Instruction

One thing that influenced the way I taught kindergarten was the memory of my favorite elementary school teacher. Mrs. Hilton, my sixth-grade teacher, was an older lady with a cloud of silver hair worn in a French roll. I think her methods were ahead of her time. Thematic instruction and experiential education were just gaining popularity when I was in college, but I had already experienced them firsthand in the sixth grade.

Let me tell you a little about her classroom. Jefferson Elementary in Pasadena was an old two-story stone building. All the rooms had been constructed with a cloak room at one end, a feature undoubtedly handy for a colder climate where weather necessitates a space for a plethora of jackets, raincoats, hats, scarfs, and boots; but not much needed in Southern California. Nevertheless, Mrs. Hilton made good use of it. Since the sixth-grade social studies unit was South America, she turned the cloak room into a Spanish hacienda. She covered the front wall of it with brown wrapping paper on which she painted a tile roof, wooden beams, windows, and a climbing bougainvillea vine. In the classroom, she did away with the usual neat rows of desks and instead placed worktables around the edges. Bulletin boards were covered with maps and pictures of South America.

Every day after lunch she would read aloud from a chapter book called, *Louisa and the Butterfly Shawl*, about a girl in South America. Whenever she stopped, we wished she would just keep on reading. One day she introduced a new craft project for the girls, presenting each of us with a large square of white cotton fabric, recycled from old bedsheets. It was our job to make a shawl by first coloring designs with crayons, pressing down heavily to cause the wax to build up. Next, she dipped our shawls into tubs of Rit dye to alter the background color. All the other girls in the class decorated their cloth with pretty flowers, but I chose to cover mine with brightly colored butterflies. I chose blue dye to make the background look like sky. For the final touch, she had each of us use a pin to painstakingly pull threads to fringe around the perimeter of our shawls. The results were beautiful.

There were other crafts that went with the theme. The boys learned how to braid strips of leather into a lariat, like a vaquero on the pampas of Argentina. We all made *cascarones* by blowing out eggs, painting them, and filling the interior with carefully cut perfumed confetti, then sealing them. We learned songs and folk dances. The themed curriculum encompassed many interdisciplinary learnings combining literature, art, writing, music, and dance.

Toward the end of the year, we held a fiesta for the parents. This involved writing and acting in a play, our version of the chapter book. I was thrilled when I was chosen to play the part of Louisa, because of my butterfly shawl. When the parent day came, we produced our play in front of the hacienda backdrop. We sang songs and did dances that required the use of maracas and castanets. Refreshments were served and we happily followed the custom of breaking our perfumed cascarones above the heads of our friends.

Of course, this experience-driven curriculum inspired me to be interested in learning more about South America. I can still picture the blank test maps of South America with outlines of the countries and how quickly we could fill in all the names. That information stuck with me. Mrs. Hilton made learning interesting and fun.

When I began teaching kindergarten, I tried to follow her example. Since the district curriculum guide began with first grade, I was left free to choose what to present. Starting every Spring, I would select an instructional theme for the remainder of the school year. I always did a mural that covered a whole wall of the room, just like Mrs. Hilton had. It created a colorful new environment. I generally painted the background and then displayed the children's work on it. The children did daily arts and crafts projects that went with our theme. The walls were covered with photos to provide visual instruction. I read thematic books at story time. The bookshelves were stocked with related picture books. We learned songs and dances that went with our unit of study. As a culmination we did a related field trip, often going to a museum, a fire station, the zoo, the farm at the fairgrounds or the nearby ocean.

Over the years I chose many different themes, sometimes repeating my favorites. Some of the ones I remember are the circus, dinosaurs, transportation, community helpers, space, Mexico, It's a Small World, the zoo, the farm, and the ocean. Each time the environment in our room transformed to reflect what we were learning about, and our activities centered around that theme. The themes usually led up to Open House near the end of the school year.

However, all year long our room environment and curriculum activities were also centered around the theme of the seasons. In the fall we studied nocturnal animals, spiders, deciduous trees, and harvest. In winter we learned about types of weather, hibernation, etc. In spring the life cycles of frogs, butterflies, and other signs of the seasons. I tried to make learning an interesting and memorable experience for the children.

I am looking back over the trail of years and recalling my job. I started so long ago, but a surprising thing happened recently. Someone forwarded an online posting to me. It posed the question, "Who was your favorite teacher?" I thought once again about Mrs. Hilton. Then I began to read the answers. Most people recalled and named a high school or college teacher of math, art, biology and so on. Locations mentioned were in the district where I formerly taught. Some just posted a name. I was suddenly surprised to see my former married name posted there. I only taught in that location back in the 1960s. I was amazed! I was someone's favorite teacher. Whoever remembers kindergarten?

Teaching is like walking with children along an upward path. As you progress, one step at a time, you may pick up pebbles and toss them into a quiet lake. They disappear but leave behind ripples of remembrance that keep moving outward in ever widening circles. A wonderful thing about teaching is those ripples. You never know how far they will reach. I think Mrs. Hilton would be surprised that over seventy years later I am recalling and imitating her teaching methods. It is also satisfying to me that, out there somewhere, there is a man in his sixties that still remembers kindergarten! Perhaps there is a recurring theme here that the learning environment of childhood can leave an indelible impression.

Our Ocean Theme

A Room for All Seasons

Fall

Winter

Spring

Lindy and the Angel

A mother came in for a parent conference on the first day of the school year. She wanted to let me know that their religious beliefs would preclude her daughter from participating in some of our kindergarten activities. "She may stand during the flag salute, but she may not salute or say the pledge of allegiance," she informed me.

I think she expected me to object and seemed prepared to argue. "That will be alright," I said. "Our country's founders felt it was important that people be free to follow their own religious beliefs."

"Also, she is not allowed to participate in some holiday activities," her mother stated. "She will know which ones are O.K. for her to do."

Some kindergarteners would use that as an excuse to not do any projects so I was a little concerned that the daughter might prove lazy. But, I needn't have worried. Lindy was a capable student eager to learn. As five- year-olds go, she was tall, slender, and serious in her demeanor. She appeared closer to the six-year-old end of the kindergarten age spectrum. She had very pretty glossy black hair that hung straight to the middle of her back. It was unique in that there was a narrow stripe of pure white in her hair. Her mother said she had had it since birth. Lindy was bright and very verbal, fluent in English and Spanish.

As we got into Fall activities, she never hesitated about what projects she could and could not do. She was emphatic that it was O.K. to paint a picture of a pumpkin growing on a vine but making a paper jack-o-lantern was off limits, as were ghosts or witches, but autumn leaves were fine. She had clearly defined ideas and would frequently inform me of which things were acceptable to Jehovah and which were not. She was very enthusiastic about school and happily joined in most things that we did.

She was also very outspoken. One day as the group was sitting on the rug she raised her hand. When I called on her she said in a firm loud voice, "Jehovah hates drugs! Doesn't he teacher?"

I answered carefully as I didn't want any little parrots going home and saying that teacher was telling them what Jehovah liked or didn't like. Her statement had come out of the blue. I hedged, "What makes you say that, Lindy?"

"My mommy said so!" I nodded and decided now was a good time to dismiss the class to go outside for recess. Lindy however followed me over to my desk. She obviously had more to say now that the other children were out on the playground. "My mommy says alcohol is a drug! Jehovah hates alcohol because it makes people do bad things."

I paid more attention. "Did something bad happen Lindy?"

She hesitated and looked at me with a serious expression on her little face. "My daddy had too much alcohol last night and he was yelling at my mommy."

"Did he hurt you honey?" it was my responsibility to ask.

"No, he was only mad at mommy, but I had to call 9-1-1." For the first time she looked uncertain, like she wasn't sure if that had been the right thing to do or not. "He had a knife," she explained.

When her mother came to pick her daughter up after school I verified what had happened the night before. The mom said that the dad was indeed in jail. It had not been a made-up story. "Sometimes he gets too drunk," the mom said in explanation.

"Lindy was just trying to help." I was glad he was in the custody of the authorities as it meant for at least temporary safety.

As we entered December there were many projects that Lindy refused to do. She did make a snow-covered pine tree but Santa and Rudolph, a stocking, and other holiday crafts were declined. That's why I was so surprised one day to see her hard at work on an angel. The children always enjoyed this activity. The free-standing angel had a skirt made of an inverted cone of stiff white paper which the kids covered with pretty designs in soft pastel colors. The other piece consisted of the angel's face and wings inserted into the top of the cone and the finishing fancy touch was a bit of gold paper doily attached below her face. I watched as Lindy cut carefully around the wings. She concentrated as she used a new pink crayon on the angel's cheeks. She took her time making a border of light blue stars around the bottom of the skirt. She used yellow for the halo but not for the hair, as many of the children were doing. She made the hair long and black but left a streak of white.

As I added glitter to her angel I complimented her, "You did your best coloring on this Lindy and how nice she turned out."

She smiled shyly, "I really like how pretty she is!" When it was dismissal time that day I began to pass out the projects to go home. Lindy carried her angel carefully over to my desk. "Here," she said, "she is a present for you."

"Oh, Lindy I couldn't keep your lovely angel. You should take her home to live at your house. You worked so hard on her," I said.

Lindy seemed to waver for a minute but then she said thoughtfully, "Teacher, I know that angels are real. They are in the Bible, so I made her. But I don't think my mom would let me keep her. She says Jehovah doesn't like Christmas decorations.

I looked at her sad little face and thought for a minute. I said, "I have an idea, Lindy." One of the parents had donated a small live fir tree for our classroom. It sat on top of a round table in the center of our room. We had decorated it with paper chains and popcorn strings. "What if we put your angel on our classroom tree?" She liked that idea and beamed as I placed her angel on the very top. "Thank you, Lindy." I said, "She is so beautiful."

It was later in the school year that Lindy and her mother fled without notice to the shelter of family in Mexico. I missed having her in our class but hoped that she had now found safety and a peaceful life.

Every Christmas after that there was a glittering angel on the top of our classroom tree, a beautiful angel with blue stars on her skirt and black hair with a white streak.

Gerardo

By the time I retired, I had taught hundreds of children. As important as each of them is during the school year when you are together, the truth is, with the passing of time their memories blend together, except for a few who for one reason or another stand out as unforgettable. One of those was a boy named Gerardo. It was in my last year of teaching that one night my husband and I went to a western themed dinner and square dance. Duane happily wore his boots and cowboy hat. We ate baked beans, spicy barbeque sauce, cold slaw and corn bread dripping with butter. To vigorously mix it all up, we promenaded our partner and do-si-doed for the rest of the evening.

I went to bed exhausted. After a couple hours I woke up with nausea and stomach pain. After throwing up repeatedly I kept thinking I should feel better. Not so. In the morning I still felt terrible with severe pain. My husband insisted I go to our doctor. Since I had a sneaking suspicion, I was dying, I agreed. I told the doctor about the spicy, greasy menu and the dancing, but assured him that I only had sodas to drink. I said, "I know its January and flu is going around, but the thing is, I never get the flu".

He was palpating my stomach and pressed hard on one spot. "Ouch!" I yelped, ready to jump off the exam table.

"No," he smiled. "I don't think you have the flu. I think you need surgery!" After an ultrasound proved him right, I checked into Hoag Hospital to have my gall bladder removed. Because of complications, I ended up spending five days there. The doctor said I needed to spend another few days off work to rest up from peritonitis. I hadn't planned on being out that long. Even with the Martin Luther King Jr. holiday giving me an extra day off, I needed to make more lesson plans for the sub. My husband agreed to deliver them to my classroom.

Upon arriving at the school, he noticed a police car in the parking lot. He naturally assumed it was there as part of the police D.A.R.E. program but decided to have a little fun when he walked into the school office. "O.K. which one of you is getting arrested?" he quipped.

He was the one surprised when they answered, "They are in your wife's class!" The police were called for one of my students named Gerardo.

"You called the cops on a kindergartner?" Duane asked, totally amazed.

The secretary nodded. I got the full story when I returned to work a few days later. The account I received was that Gerardo had been arguing with a little girl in the class. When he picked up a metal chair to throw it at her, the sub intervened and confiscated the chair. At this point he began screaming and lashing out. She tried to restrain him and called out for the other kindergarten teacher in the adjoining room. That teacher, Miss A., was a former Special Ed. Teacher, so she offered to hold him while the sub phoned for help. The office sent the custodian, a strong man, over to the classroom and he put the tantrum thrower over his shoulder and carried him off to the office.

The drama did not end there. The sub sustained long fingernail scratches down both arms, which were bleeding profusely. Although trained in how to hold him, Miss A. had still been bitten on one arm. She had been wearing a jeans jacket of heavy denim, yet she showed me the still visible puncture wounds, a perfect circle of red marks showing where all his little teeth had managed to perforate her skin despite the jacket. It looked worse than a dog bite. The custodian also did not escape. He suffers from back pain and Gerardo, although slung over his shoulder, managed to keep kicking him hard with his heavy boots all the way over to the office. That was when the police were called. Because of the risk of hepatitis and aids or back injury, all three of the victims were sent for medical care, including tetanus shots for the teachers. Subs had to be hired to fill in for the afternoon in both kindergartens.

Gerardo had been in trouble before, though on a milder level. On several occasions the other kindergarten teachers and the aide had to bench him at recess for hitting other children. The odd thing was, although I was informed about his difficulties on the playground, he always behaved himself for me. In fact, he seemed anxious for my approval.

The principal called the parents into her office and met with them. Gerardo was suspended for a few days and only allowed to return to class when they agreed to take him to regular consultations with a psychiatric counselor. This was arranged free of cost to them through social services. Meanwhile, he continued to behave for me in class. One day, the noon duty supervisor sent him to the office for vicious fighting at lunch time. Again, the principal suspended him for a couple days. I conferenced again with the parents. The mother complained about the psychologist and was adamant that her son had no problems. Gerardo, a tall handsome child was from her prior marriage and she was very permissive with him. I think she wanted to be the favored parent in the divorce, a recipe for trouble. The stepfather meekly spoke up and offered to take the boy to the counseling sessions. She promptly shut him down. I encouraged them to keep on attending. Perhaps it would be alright anyway since Gerardo tended to come unglued only when I was not around. He seemed to respond to gentle guidance from me, or so I thought.

I had returned to work with a permission note from my doctor, but with the proviso that I not lift anything heavier than a gallon of milk for at least a month. One day my class was having a particularly busy day and was behind schedule for getting to recess. It was time for recess, but the children were taking forever to clean up the room, pieces of games were scattered all around the rug. I was trying to rush them along by dismissing one at a time to go outside. Gerardo was dragging his feet about helping two other boys with the Legos. When I dismissed one of them to recess, Gerardo got mad, picked up the large plastic box of Legos, threw it on the floor and began kicking them. Hundreds of Legos flew across the carpet!

I was extremely annoyed with his outburst of temper. Instead of my usual soft way of dealing with him I reacted with immediate discipline. I said firmly, "Gerardo, you will not go out to recess until you have picked up every single Lego!"

"He needs to pick them up too! He was playing with them too," he shouted pointing at the other boy.

"No," I said and sent the other boy outside. "You were the one who threw the box so _you_ will pick them all up."

At this point Gerardo began attacking me. He was not used to consequences.

Did I mention that this happened to be a day when my husband was volunteering in my classroom? As I was holding a kicking screaming Gerardo at arms' length to guard my still healing stomach, I looked up to see a glaring Duane rushing towards us ready to protect his wife. "Oh no," I thought. "I don't need him to touch the child." I said firmly, "Stop! Please just call the office." I assured him I was fine and held Gerardo at bay until the custodian arrived.

The principal went with three strikes and you're out. On learning that the parents had stopped taking Gerardo to the psychologist, (because mom didn't think he needed it,) he was expelled for the rest of the school year. Whereupon, the parents enrolled him in another school that would understand him better.

Like I said, the memory of some children sticks in your mind. Gerardo was the only student I ever had suspended from my class, or expelled from school, and although I was not there to see it, my only kindergartner to have the police called on him.

Valentines

One of my favorite days in kindergarten was Valentine's Day. Beginning the first of February, we began finding out about how a post office works and constructing a pretend one in our room. We would watch a movie on how mail is processed and delivered. The children made mail trucks from construction paper with wheels that turned. They memorized their addresses and wrote letters to mail home. In our fake post office was a toy cash register and play money. The kids could buy stamps (my saved Easter seals) and use them to put on pretend mail they wrote. Two children at a time were allowed to use rubber stamps and ink pads and cancel the mail. The post office unit led up to February 14th and the delivery of valentines.

In preparation for this, each child brought a shoe box to school. I covered the boxes and lids separately in white butcher paper and cut a large slit in the top of each one. The children each took a turn at the art table where they decorated their box. They could choose whatever they wanted from an assortment of red and pink paper hearts, shiny foil stickers, small paper lace doilies, and then add silver or gold glitter.

Next, I pasted a tiny student photo of each child onto a sheet of paper, printed their name underneath it and made enough photocopies of the page for each child to take one home along with instructions for their parents. Their homework was to cut the page apart and glue a picture onto the front of each valentine card they wished to bring to school. Meanwhile I cut my page and affixed a picture to the front of each shoe box, arranging the boxes in alphabetical order on the shelves of a bookcase in our post office. When the children brought their valentines to class, they could take a turn in the post office and cancel their valentines with a heart shaped rubber stamp in red ink and pop each card into the shoebox with a matching name and picture. This worked well, even for the non-readers.

On Valentine's Day we held a simple party. The children frosted and decorated heart shaped sugar cookies and then sat at colorful placemats they had made. They enjoyed a heart cookie, tiny candy hearts with words on them, and a cup of red punch. Finally came the best part. I passed out the shoeboxes and they all lifted the lids at once to look at the valentines they had received.

This was the most memorable time for me, as I listened to the "oohs" and "aahs" and comments of delight. There was laughter at the funny cards. "Oh, this one has a silly puppy on it!"

"Mine has a kitty with a heart nose!"

"Look, this one has googly eyes that really move!"

"This one is so pretty and shiny!" This experience was a first for all of them. The room positively bubbled over with pleasure. Now that I am retired, the 14th of February is much like every other day. It is the day when I miss kindergarten the most.

That system of delivering valentines was the result of years of modifying my method. When I first started teaching kindergarten in 1962, I had begun by using a valentine box, the system I had experienced when I was in elementary school. I remember when I was in the sixth grade, we had a big, decorated box that sat in the front of the room. You made valentine cards at home and brought them to school to drop into the box. There were not usually enough cards for everyone in the large class. You put the names of your best friends on the cards, plus, if you had the courage, one with the name of the boy you thought was the cutest. The downside to this system was that some people got more cards than others. It had the potential effect of hurt feelings.

In kindergarten I asked each child to bring enough cards for the entire class but 30 kids bringing 30 valentines meant 900 cards being passed out by non-readers. It was chaos. Gradually I modified it to bringing a packet of cards with no names on the front and kids sitting in a circle while one child walked around and passed out his packet of cards. That was time consuming, but at least it worked until I finally came up with the post office and individual boxes.

Before I started teaching kindergarten, my husband and I would live with his parents over summer vacation, to save money while he was in medical school. My mother-in-law, Marion, was a kindergarten teacher. One summer day she planned a project for us. She rummaged around in her garage and found a large square box with a separate lid. "You will need a valentine box," she said.

The afternoon that followed was a thoroughly enjoyable one. We sat at the wooden picnic table, with a pitcher of ice-cold lemonade, under the shade of a sprawling old tree, to create a valentine box. After covering the box with plain white shelf paper, we began cutting hearts from pink and red construction paper and scraps of shiny foil gift wrap and glued them on. Next, we added lacy paper doilies and valentine stickers and glitter. When we were done it was a thing of beauty ready for future use.

Remember Marion was the person who made me want to become a kindergarten teacher. Marion had inspired me with a visit to her kindergarten classroom. I had changed my major to education and graduated from U.C.L.A. with a degree and a teaching credential all because of a spark Marion had ignited.

She was a great mentor for teaching ideas, always showing me a new craft project, or teaching me a poem, song or fingerplay for kindergarten. She would set up art projects in the yard for us to do together for our classrooms. We made musical instruments, papier mache Humpty Dumptys, decorated Easter eggs, puppets, and other fun things on those summer afternoons.

To go with the valentine box, she taught me a little poem:

Five little valentines were having a race.

The first little valentine had a funny face.

The second little valentine was covered with lace.

The third little valentine said, "I love you."

The fourth little valentine said, "I do too."

The fifth little valentine was sly as a fox

And he ran the fastest to the valentine box!

We made stick puppets to go with it out of tongue depressors. The children could each hold a decorated heart puppet, say their line aloud, and have great fun racing to the box.

For over twenty years Marion was a wonderful resource and we often chatted about kindergarten, even after she retired. When she was hospitalized with ovarian cancer, my son and I went to visit her in the hospital. She did not look good. The next day I called her on the telephone. I wanted to tell her I knew I was lucky to have such a great mother-in-law who had taught for thirty-five years, and I thanked her for helping me to decide on kindergarten teaching. We began to reminisce about some of our projects, laughing about them. "Oh, just a minute," she said, "the nurse is here to give me a pain shot. It's been getting worse."

"Are you still O.K. to talk? "I asked after a moment

"Yes," she continued weakly, "Do you remember the valentine box?" We both could recall that fun summer day like it was yesterday. After a few minutes the morphine began to make her speech slower. Her mind began to wander. The painkiller was taking effect. "Oh, look at all those colors on the valentine box…and the hearts are moving…that one has a funny face, and that one is…" her voice trailed off.

No one else would have understood what she was talking about, but remembering the rhyme, I completed her sentence, "covered with lace."

"Yes," she breathed, "and that one says…" there was a pause.

"I love you!" I said with tears in my eyes. There was no sound on the other end of the phone. "Marion?" I asked.

Finally, she answered, "I do too." Only silence followed. I didn't want to hang up. I didn't want to break the connection. After a long time, I put the receiver down softly. She died later that night. Her mind had been in the world of kindergarten until the final hours of her life.

She had certainly passed along that passion. I taught on and off (with childbearing breaks) over a stretch of forty-three years. My daughter also became a kindergarten teacher and has been doing it for well over twenty years so far. I think Marion knew she was leaving an ongoing legacy.

I thought once again about the heart puppets racing to the valentine box. They had words written on them, words that need to be said. In fact, words from the heart were what the valentine box was all about. It was the keeper of the words: words of affirmation, words of friendship, words of love, and when the box was opened the words would flood the room, filling it with warm feelings that floated in the air to become favorite memories of the world of kindergarten.

The Language Barrier

In order to be rehired after my years of substituting I had worked to get certified as a language development specialist. After I came to Wilson, I had reason to be glad I had done that. It was useful. In an area of recent immigrants, language acquisition was a very important aspect of teaching. Almost all my students were learning English as a second language. For a while Wilson was a bilingual school as our numbers of Spanish speakers was high. The few children I had that spoke languages other than Spanish: Japanese, Vietnamese, Russian and Tagalog, were all able to speak English as well. That was not the case with Frank.

Frank enrolled weeks after school had begun. He came with his father who told me that they had just moved here from China. He explained that Frank had been raised in China with his mother and grandmother and did not yet speak a word of English. He was bringing him today, but his mother would be doing so from now on.

The little boy before me was pale and obviously frightened. He didn't cry but I think he was close to it. He was standing stiffly at attention with his mouth set in a straight line, bravely ready to face anything this strange place had to offer. Something about the expression on his little round face made my heart just melt. "Come," I said and took his hand. I ushered a quiet, frightened Frank into the room, and introduced him to the other children. "This is our new friend, Frank. You can help show him where things are in our classroom. He just moved here from a country called China and he doesn't understand any English yet."

Juan raised his hand, "Does he speak Spanish?"

"No," I said. "He speaks only Chinese but after a while he will learn to talk to you." The class seemed satisfied with that answer. After all, many of them had only been learning English since the beginning of the school year. For most of them Spanish was their first language. Of course, the transition was easier for them because they could speak to their friends to be understood and when needed I could offer explanations in Spanish. They probably assumed teacher could speak any language. But just as Frank could not speak any English, I knew not a word of Chinese! This was going to be a challenge.

On the second day of school, Frank arrived with his mother, a very pretty lady. She had limited English but nodded and smiled at me a lot. She was proud and pleased as she told me, "He know one-word English now." Then she bent over and said something to him in Chinese. It did not need translation. She was obviously telling him to say his one word of English for the teacher.

Obediently Frank stood at attention, looked up at me and barked out one word quite clearly, "NO!" To my credit I think, I did not laugh, just clapped. He was very proud of his new word, and meanwhile I thought that he would probably get a lot of use out of that one.

The challenge began when it was writing time. I had made each child a journal by stapling sheets of blank paper inside a colorful piece of construction paper. Each day they would draw a picture and write a word underneath. When the other children went to sit at the tables I handed Frank a new journal and a box of crayons. He looked at me questioningly with both hands held out with palms up. How I wished I spoke Chinese. I pointed to him and pantomimed that he should draw himself. He immediately sat down and began doing that. When he finished, he came up to me with a neatly colored picture of himself, I pointed to it and said, "Frank," and wrote his name underneath it. He nodded his understanding, like now it made sense. The following day at journal time he went right to work. The new drawing, he brought me, showed a tiny Frank again, flanked by a tall man on one side and a lady on the other. Again, he made the palms up questioning sign. I pointed once more and wrote Dad, Frank, Mom. He positively beamed as he repeated all three words. And so, it went. The next day there were the three figures in front of a house. Next, there was a tree. I kept saying and writing the words as he delightedly repeated them. His vocabulary was increasing. He could flip back through the journal and name every word.

I usually sent home a simple page of homework, perhaps rhyming words or words that begin with a certain sound. Apparently, these pages were not understood, but Frank wanted to bring homework in. One day he brought in a whole page of completed math problems. The problems were written out by his father, (who by the way was a P.H.D. in mathematics.) Answers were written in large childish numerals. I checked them and then drew a happy face! I was surprised as they were all three-digit multiplication problems. I had never encountered a kindergartner capable of that. I tested him with a couple more problems of my own to check his ability. He quickly wrote out the answers and smiled up at me. It just confirmed how bright he was!

Frank was sometimes frustrated, often stubbornly using his word, "No" with the other children and stomping his foot. One day in the middle of free choice time I happened to look out the window to see Frank on the far side of the playground struggling to open the latch on the gate. I had not seen him slip out the door. I ran across the playground just as he managed to get the gate to the sidewalk open. I grabbed him and carried him back into the classroom. Of course, he could not tell me what was wrong, but tears were rolling down his red and blotchy cheeks. I called the office and asked if there was anyone at the school who could speak Chinese. I really needed a translator. They located a fifth grader who came and spoke with Frank who let loose with a torrent of Chinese.

"Where was he going?" I asked the translator. He said he had decided to go home. I was horrified, picturing him attempting to cross the very busy intersection. What if I had not looked up in time? "What was he so upset about?" I asked.

The fifth grader answered, "He says that some of the boys in this class are not gentlemen!" Finally, Frank calmed down, seemingly satisfied that at least someone in his school could speak Chinese. I had a subsequent talk with the boys about sharing toys, but I worried about how isolated he must feel, unable to understand English. The lack of ability to communicate was a barrier to making friends.

Most of the time Frank was very solemn and obedient. He watched the other children, followed along, doing whatever they did. The children in the class were usually patient with him. They would show him where the games were kept. He sat and shared the box of Legos with them and seemed to enjoy that. One of the girls in the class especially seemed to take him under her wing. Lindy was mature and tall for kindergarten. Her favorite pastime was to pretend she was the teacher and "read" stories to the other kids. Frank was attentive and watched the pictures. Lindy took an interest in Frank and would take him by the hand and shepherd him to the next activity.

A gap in communication came when it was time to do valentines. I had sent home a page of specific instructions about how to put valentines in envelopes and paste a picture of a classmate on the front. After school his embarrassed mother asked, "What is Valentine?" I tried to explain the custom. I told her they were little cards that said nice things to their friends, and she could find them at many stores. Apparently, I did not explain very well, or she didn't understand.

On Valentine's Day, Frank showed up with a stack of legal sized envelopes. They did have photos correctly pasted on the front, but in lieu of a valentine card, they each contained a formal letter laboriously typed and folded and saying something nice. Mine read, "*This is my best wishes to you on this special occasion. Happy Valentine's Day. Your friend,*" it was signed in careful letters, Frank. I asked his mother if he did them by himself and she nodded, "He take very long time!"

Every day after school Frank's mom was waiting on the bench outside my door. The other mothers would be chatting together in Spanish. She just sat there quietly and would nod shyly in my direction. How isolating for her to be unable to communicate with them. I would show her some of Frank's work, but we couldn't converse much. On the other hand, Frank's English was progressing by leaps and bounds. When I mentioned that to his mother she said, "Sometime he only like talk English." I thought she looked a little sad about that.

Frank continued to blossom. His vocabulary increased daily, not only in English but in Spanish as well. He could count in Spanish and say the days of the week. One day I was dismissing the kids to recess in Spanish. I let the girls go first but a couple boys stood up. Frank was indignant. "*Sientate*! She said, *ninas*, not *ninos*," he corrected.

By March the solemn little boy had become a joyful one. He loved school and participating in all our activities. I have a picture of a laughing Frank wearing butterfly wings when we learned about metamorphosis. In another photo an amazed Frank is holding a live rock crab that he caught on our field trip to the beach. He was learning to talk with other children on the playground. The language barrier was coming down.

One Monday near the end of the year, Frank's father again brought him to school. While Frank played outside, his father asked if he could come into the classroom and speak with me privately. I could tell something was wrong by the look on his face. In a broken voice he told me that Frank's mother was dead. "Oh no," I cried, "she was here on Friday afternoon, and she looked fine." I couldn't believe what I was hearing.

His eyes filled with tears as he said, "She committed suicide on Friday night." "Frank doesn't know," he said. "I told him she was sick and had to go to the hospital. Please don't say anything to him yet. I will wait to tell him." Of course, I expressed my sorrow at his terrible loss. I was in shock when he left. I pictured the pretty young mom waiting outside my room each day, unable to say a word to the other moms who were chatting in Spanish. She was in a strange land, with her only child rapidly becoming comfortable in an unfamiliar language. Whatever emotion had motivated her action it was must have been compounded by loneliness and a sense of isolation.

Frank was absent for a couple days and when he returned his grandmother, newly arrived from China, picked him up. A couple days went by. I still didn't know if they had told him yet. Then one day I noticed Frank talking with Lindy. They appeared to be arguing. A minute later Lindy marched over to me and was very indignant as she said, "Teacher, Frank said his mommy is an angel now. That is not true! Everybody knows you have to be dead to be an angel, right?" She continued, "I see his mom lots of times when she comes to pick him up."

Now I had my answer. Frank had been told. I replied carefully, "Lindy I am sad to tell you that his mommy did die." Not all five-year-old would be able to understand that news but she did. Lindy immediately turned and walked across the room to where Frank stood stiffly with his fists clenched and his mouth set in a tight line. He was bravely ready to do battle with anyone who challenged his mom's angel status. My eyes filled with tears as I witnessed the most touching moment I have ever seen. That compassionate little girl simply threw her arms around Frank and hugged him. While he began to sob with grief on her shoulder, she just gently patted his back and comforted that motherless child. Michelangelo could perhaps have done justice to portray the beauty of that scene. I cannot. There is no way to describe that poignant moment. There are no words, not in any language.

The Number Line

When I first got my own room at Wilson School, I adopted an idea I had seen in classrooms where I substituted. Several teachers used a number line. They posted a number on the wall for each day of attendance, usually using index cards or a little slip of paper for each number. I decided to copy the idea but tweak it a little.

At the school supply shop, I discovered a huge selection of small tablets of sticky post-it notes that came in different colors and shapes. I purchased a dozen. On the first day of school I showed the children a little tablet of bright red apples, "This is number one," I said as I wrote the numeral with a bold black felt pen. "I am going to put it where we can see it and always remember the very first day that we came to kindergarten." I tore off the sticky note and placed the little apple on the wooden bulletin board frame that encircled the room.

One of the curriculum goals on the report card for kindergarten is to learn to recognize numbers one through thirty. Each day I introduced another numeral and added another red apple to our wall. Some children could recognize the numbers up to ten; others not yet, especially in my class, where many students were hearing them in English for the first time. After nine days the kids were used to the routine of adding a red apple and then counting them aloud. On day ten I said, "I have a surprise today, instead of an apple we are going to put something different on our number line." I pulled out a tablet of yellow stars and wrote a ten. "Number ten is special because it has a zero! When we are counting, and we see a zero let's give a happy clap." We practiced counting and giving a clap.

As September progressed, our number line began to grow, a tidy line, like a little train following the wooden track across the front of our room. It was a good tool for teaching math, as more children began passing their number recognition assessments. On the first day of October we talked about the new month, and I surprised them by changing to a tablet of bright orange pumpkins. In November we switched to a light brown maple leaf. By then our line had reached across the large bulletin board and was approaching the corner of the room. I stopped using my yardstick as we counted and switched to using a laser pointer as the line turned the corner. December brought green pine trees followed by white snowflakes in January. Along with the names of numerals we were also learning the months of the year.

In February we began adding red hearts. The long line was interspersed by now with several yellow stars, one for each time we came to a zero. The children chanted the numbers every day, clapping each time we reached a zero. They learned to count by tens with the stars. Sometimes we also counted in Spanish. Since they all spoke Spanish as their first language, I thought we might as well learn to count in both languages.

February was special because we were nearing day 100. Being able to rote count to 100 is also a math goal for kindergarten. The whole school celebrated day 100. Zero the Hero came to our room dressed in a superhero costume with a cape and a big 100 on his chest. After he came flying in, he helped us count our number line until we reached the extra-large star with gold sparkle on it to celebrate two zeros. All the children brought a baggy of 100 small food items to share. We sat around a large white tablecloth while they counted out ten piles of Cheerios, M and M's, Skittles, raisins, and so on. After each counted ten piles of ten they had a better visual concept of a hundred.

Then we shook the tablecloth to mix everything together. Everyone could then fill a plastic cup of the trail mix of treats.

The children were learning from the number line. Perhaps I was too. I remember one day right after dismissal just standing there and really staring at those numbers. It was close to the end of the school year and the line was nearing completion. The colorful parade gaily marched across the front of the room, turned the corner, traversed the width of the big room and was approaching the far corner. The red hearts of February had morphed into the green frogs of March and the pink rabbits of April led to the lavender butterflies of May. So far, only a couple light blue fish signaled June. The end was inexorably approaching. I glanced with nostalgia back at that first little red apple with the number one on it and felt a lump in my throat. The last day of school would be here soon.

There are 184 instructional days in a school year so I know in advance where the line will end. I stopped to think. It occurred to me that those are not just school days represented there on the wall. Those are days of my life. They are gone and will not come again. I studied the length of that parade. I wondered how many more days are left to me. Of course, only God knows that. I recalled a Bible verse from Psalms: So, teach us to number our days, that we may apply our hearts unto wisdom. What was I being taught by those numbered days? Does applying the heart unto wisdom mean following my heart to make wise choices?

It was in that moment that I finally reached an important decision on how to use the days left to me. I walked over to the principal's office to inform her that I had decided to retire!

Jesus

It was during my tenth year at Wilson school that I began mulling over the idea of retirement. It was not an easy decision. There were pros and cons to weigh. On the side of continuing to work, the biggest factor was that I loved my job. I would miss it if I left. For the past three years I had finally acquired what I considered the perfect circumstances for teaching kindergarten.

I had been given one of the two large rooms located in the separate kindergarten building. I did not have to share it with another teacher. There was lots of space to store all my materials. The room adjoined a separate kindergarten yard to which I had a key, so I could safely work as late as I wanted. Another satisfying thing was that it allowed the class schedule to be an Early Bird/Late Owl one. The ratio of students per teacher was currently capped at 20 to 1. Twenty students in a class is an ideal number. Ten students come for the first hour, then the entire class for the main part of the day, only ten students remained after the lunch break. It was a wonderful schedule which allowed me to run small groups during the split time giving each child more attention.

However, there were factors weighing in on the side of retirement. My husband had retired from his job and was at home all day. It would be nice to be with him and be free to travel. At almost sixty-four, I was the oldest employee on staff. Age is just a number, but still. Also, part way through the school year Measure A was passed; the funds would allow our school to be remodeled over the summer. It meant that the kindergarten building was scheduled to be gutted. I would need to box up all my personal teaching materials and furniture and store them over the summer, and then cart them back again in the fall. That seemed like a lot of extra work for perhaps just another year or two before retirement. I wavered about which side of the question to land on.

Meanwhile, my husband decided to volunteer in my classroom. He came in to help with all sorts of things: oiling the bikes, replacing a broken pedal, playing ball at recess, passing out supplies, reaching the tops of bulletin boards, etc. The most valuable thing he did was during the split hour when I worked with a reading group. He would supervise the remaining table of five children in another activity. He was very outgoing and fun, and the children responded to having a man helper. They loved it when he came, especially one little boy named Jesus. I would describe Jesus as habitually sweet, social, and always smiling.

He would ask me almost daily if Mr. M. was coming and was excited if I said that he was. At the beginning of the year I had tested all of the children to see which alphabet letters they could recognize. Jesus had only been able to identify one, letter S. He also could not write his name, making only a string of odd little spirals resembling snails. One day about mid-year he proudly showed my husband his current test results. He had finally learned to identify all of the letters and tell what sound each of them made. Duane praised him for his achievement, gave him a high five and said, "Jesus, you are my man!" Jesus was so happy he was beaming all day.

Like all the children in this class, Jesus spoke Spanish as his first language, but he was also fluent in English. Sometimes he translated for other children in the class. He was aware that not everyone understood English, but one day as he was working with Mr. M., he said something to my husband in Spanish. Duane told him, "I don't understand Spanish." Jesus asked him why. Duane explained, "Well where I grew up no one spoke Spanish." Jesus was dumbfounded at the idea that there were some people who could not speak Spanish.

"But Spanish is easy!" he said. He quietly thought about it for a while with a troubled look on his face and then said, "Mr. M., can you say, ay yi yi?"

With a straight face Duane said, "Ay, yi, yi!"

Jesus cracked a big smile and said, "See Mr. M. you <u>can</u> speak Spanish!"

Duane never stopped laughing about that.

On another day Jesus showed Duane how well he could write his name now, and, in an effort to inform Duane about the letters in his name he said, "In Spanish you say the J different, not like jam or jelly, but like Jose." That little bit of information may or may not have helped Duane. It may explain why I have kept a bedraggled valentine card tucked in my Bible for many years. The little red card with hearts says, "I love you," and underneath, printed in childish handwriting, from Jesus. I can choose how to pronounce it.

I finally made the big decision that it was time to retire, influenced partly because I wanted time to be able to travel or stay home and spend time with my husband. It had been a difficult decision, bringing with it a lot of emotion. When June came and my last day with the children finally arrived, I knew it would be bittersweet. Duane came in to help with readying the room for summer.

We played musical chairs with the class and as each chair was subtracted, we stacked it on top of the tables. When the game was over, the furniture was stored for summer. Next, the class went outside for one final recess. While I did yard duty, I gave Duane the task of taking down all the butcher paper background off the bulletin boards, to strip them.

Jesus hung back close to my husband and offered to help. "Jesus, you should go outside and play with your friends," Duane said. "It is the last time." He knew Jesus lived in an apartment building on a busy street with no yard to play in over the summer.

But Jesus was adamant, "I want to work with you."

Duane thanked him and handed down the strips of torn paper for the trash bins. "You are a big helper Jesus," he said.

Jesus smiled and said, "I know. Remember, **I'm your man!**"

Finally, the children came back inside to hear one last story and gather their things. Then, they all lined up at the door to go home. As they stood there in two neat lines, it was time to sing our goodbye song. I always choke up when I sing that song for the final time before vacation. I started doing that over forty-three years ago! Now it struck me that this would be the last time I would sing those words.

The class began to chorus:

Goodbye now, goodbye now,

The clock says we're done,

Goodbye now, goodbye now

Goodbye everyone.

As I looked at Jesus and all the other sweet little faces behind him, the tears began rolling down my cheek. Time for me to say, "Adios ninos!" When I opened the door, I was completely taken by surprise. The mothers of my class had decided to give me a goodbye luncheon. They had quickly set up the long counter outside my classroom with a lovely buffet. They invited Duane and the principal to join us in partaking of delicious enchiladas, tacos, rice, refried beans, salads, and warm tortillas. There were even homemade tamales! There was lots of laughter and happy chatter in a mixture of Spanish and English. The children sampled the cookies and cupcakes and then enjoyed the playground one last time. School was over and it was time for play, for me, and for Jesus, even though he was the man.

The following morning only staff had to attend. I just needed to complete the tasks on a final checkout list. I finished removing any personal items that were left in my classroom. For a moment I stood looking around at the bare bulletin boards, boring brown and colorless. The room contained only the stacked furniture that would be removed prior to the start of demolition. How quiet it was without the sound of children's laughter. I went over to the office to file cum folders, turn in my keys and say goodbye. On leaving, I headed across the kindergarten yard towards my parked car. Stepping onto the sidewalk I swung the gate closed behind me. As I did, I glanced back at the empty playground. It was an eerily familiar moment. Decades faded away as I recalled a long-ago memory. I have seen this picture before. With my fingers curled around the chain link gate, once again I am standing outside a kindergarten yard gazing in wistfully. There is the big shade tree sheltering a grassy lawn. There are the swings, the teeter totter, the slide. With a last look at the empty playground, I turn and walk away. I will miss that world, but I will always cherish the memories of my **life in kindergarten.**

www.ingramcontent.com/pod-product-compliance
Lightning Source LLC
LaVergne TN
LVHW072116060526
838201LV00011B/254